# AMERICAN FOLK ART
## OF THE TWENTIETH CENTURY

"Folk arts are *alive*. Indeed, in many places and among many groups, they are growing."

—BESS LOMAX HAWES
*Director of the Folk Arts Program*
*of the National Endowment*
*for the Arts*

John Cross
Figures from *America's Greatest Traveling Side Show*
1982
Carved and painted wood; the figures range in size up to 18″ high
Various private collections
Photo by Bill Buckner

# AMERICAN FOLK ART
## OF THE TWENTIETH CENTURY

### Jay Johnson

### William C. Ketchum, Jr.

Foreword by Dr. Robert Bishop

*To the people who create*

Published in the United States of America by
Rizzoli International Publications, Inc.
712 Fifth Avenue
New York, N.Y. 10019

**Library of Congress Cataloging in Publication Data**
Johnson, Jay.
　American folk art of the twentieth century.

　Includes bibliographical references.
　1. Primitivism in art—United States.　2. Art,
American.　3. Art, Modern—20th century—United States.
I. Ketchum, William C., 1931–　.　II. title.
N6512.5.P7J6　1983　　709'.2'2　[B]　　83-42934
ISBN 0-8478-0503-4

Created and produced by Cynthia Parzych Publishing, Inc.
64 West 82nd Street, New York, N.Y. 10024

*President:* Cynthia Parzych
*Senior Editor:* Jay Hyams
*Assistant Editor:* Mary Haffner
*Design:* Levavi & Levavi

Composition by Dix Type Inc., Syracuse, N.Y.
Printed and bound by Mandarin Offset International, Ltd.,
Hong Kong

# Contents

# Foreword

When I was first asked to write the foreword to this book, I expressed my unabashed enthusiasm for the project for two reasons. First, the authors are both not only recognized authorities in the field—they are also longtime friends. Second, I always enjoy the opportunity of indicating my firm belief that folk expression, though it has changed with each successive generation from the very settling of this country, continues to be a vital part of America's artistic life today.

Ever since substantial appreciation for the folk arts began just after World War I, art historians, museum curators, and collectors have waged incessant battles over what kinds of objects can properly be classified as folk.

Holger Cahill, the pioneering art historian, museum director, and curator, expressed his ideas through trailblazing exhibitions: *American Primitive Painting,* presented in 1930 at the Newark Museum, Newark, New Jersey; *American Folk Sculpture—The Work of Eighteenth and Nineteenth Century Craftsmen,* exhibited at the same museum in the fall of 1931 and winter of 1932; and *American Folk Art: The Art of the Common Man in America 1750–1900,* mounted at the Museum of Modern Art in New York City in 1932.

Cahill viewed folk art as "the unconventional side of the American tradition in the fine arts. . . . It is a varied art influenced from diverse sources, often frankly derivative, often fresh and original, and at its best an honest and straightforward expression of the story of American beginnings in the arts, and [it] is a chapter . . . in the social history of this country." He also considered folk expressions as "an overflow from the crafts." For him, folk art was "the expression of the common people, made by them and intended for their use and enjoyment. . . . While the folk art tradition has had little to do with the development of American professional art. Yet the mainstream of American art was fed by the crafts during the seventeenth, eighteenth, and early nineteenth centuries."

It is interesting to note that Cahill served as an advisor to Abby Aldrich Rockefeller, one of the great pioneering collectors. On several occasions he suggested she acquire 20th-century works as well as those from earlier periods.

Controversy about modern folk art—"primitive" works made by contemporary, self-taught artists—accelerated with the publication by the distinguished curator, art historian, and art dealer Sidney Janis in 1942 of *They Taught Themselves: American Primitive Painters of the Twentieth Century.* Conservative collectors felt that many of the artists cited by the author painted only for monetary gain and that their works were not "valid" folk art. These critics chose to forget that the greatest outpouring of folk expression—portraiture—was nearly always created for a fee and that the 18th- and 19th-century itinerant folk portraitist earned his living from his art.

In part, it is the difficulty of determining what is art that troubles the traditional folk art collector when he views 20th-century material. With historical perspective on one's side, it is much easier to look at the 18th- and 19th-century work and develop a consensus about which pieces are of significance. In the 20th century, one must rely on taste and instincts. At the same time, one must have a broad knowledge of the art world at large in order to place one's opinions about modern-day folk art in perspective. Decisions are far more difficult, and few, indeed, are brave enough to speak out with conviction.

As might be expected, not all scholars agree. Jean Lipman views folk art as "artistic efforts confined within time boundaries"—which terminate before any of the works of art illustrated in this book were created. "The signing of the Declaration of Independence in 1776 also signaled the beginning of a new independence for American art. The seeds of the native folk tradition, planted with the founding of the American colonies in the 17th century, sprouted and throve all along the eastern seaboard from the last quarter of the 18th century through the first three quarters of the

19th century. Folk art was a prime product of the new American democracy, strongly representative of the spirit of the country. By the time of the Centennial this art had reached its peak; the machine age marked the start of its decline, despite some reseeding and blossoming through the late 19th and 20th centuries."

Nina Fletcher Little, one of the early scholars in the field, sees folk art existing on many levels and in many time frames: "Two kinds of art have flourished side by side in nearly all nations. Very often their courses have run independently of each other. One we call fine art. Created by the great masters largely for the rich and ruling classes and the church, fine art served the Doges of Venice and the Kings of France. In America it served the gentry of the South and the merchant princes of New England. It was sponsored by the great families of great states.

"The other category includes American folk art. This is the art of the people—often anonymous or forgotten men and women. In the first group we see the glory and majesty of the ages. In the second we discover the character and interests of a people and the forces that molded their lives.

"American folk art is not an unskilled imitation of fine art. This must be stressed for in it lies the personal flavor of folk art. It lives in its own world and is responsive to its own surroundings. It was produced by amateurs who worked for their own gratification and the applause of their families and neighbors, and by artisans and craftsmen of varying degrees of skill and artistic sensitivity who worked for pay.

". . . It is sometimes spoken of as 'popular art,' but folk art assumes the presence of an original artist whereas popular art includes products of the printing press. Currier & Ives, for example, produced popular art. The phrase 'primitive art' is also used, but this has a wide range of meanings. It is applied to the often highly developed skills of prehistoric peoples, to the work of dedicated amateurs, and to the consciously naive style of such internationally recognized artists as the Douanier Rousseau. While all American folk art was 'provincial art' in the sense of being remote from the cultural centers of Europe, that phrase suggests rural as contrasted with urban origin, and in this sense is inexact. Folk art flourished in the towns as well as in the country and was not restricted by geographical limitations."

Herbert W. Hemphill, Jr., is certainly the most adventuresome collector and catalyst in the field in recent years. His "first" collection contained many works by the well-known, predictable painters and fine pieces of sculpture in the traditional sense. Yet, like Cahill, he has always expressed an enthusiasm for the "unconventional side."

During the last several years, his interest has focused on the modern folk artists, and he has built an important collection of their works. His book, *Twentieth Century American Folk Art and Artists*, written with Julia Weissman, celebrates the best of modern-day works. The authors' attempt to distinguish between the professional artist working deliberately within a folk tradition and the true 20th-century folk artist is interesting: "Not that the untaught artist is totally unaffected by events. On the contrary, a good many indicate a sharp awareness of them. But because such artists are not concerned with movements, fads, or theories, or the need to make a living from art, there is a direct communication between mind and hand. They are generally satisfied with whatever style or technique emerges right at the beginning. It is not the philosophy or meaning of art per se, but their own philosophies, the meaning of their own lives relative to their world and our world that concerns them. The absence of intellectualism allows for a free flow of ideation. The result is often a closer personal relationship between artist and viewer."

Two other very important collectors, authors, and scholars have caused increased public awareness for the 20th-century works. Michael Hall and Julie Hall both bring artist's eyes to their collecting. Writing in the catalog to the exhibition *American Folk Sculpture, the Personal and the Eccentric*, mounted at the Cranbrook Academy of Art Galleries, Bloomfield Hills, Michigan, Mr. Hall noted of the several 20th-century pieces in the show, ". . . this exhibition seeks to illustrate the personal and often eccentric turn of expression that the naive 'private vision' can produce. Each piece must be measured by itself and yet be seen against a backdrop of the whole history of sculpture. Against this backdrop, many of the works in the exhibition stand out as extremely vigorous in concept, daring in form, and free in execution."

The Halls' vision was once again evident in the daring exhibition *Transmitters: The Isolate Artist in America*, created by Elsa S. Weiner at the Philadelphia College of Art in 1981. The focus was on those artists whose works fit no mold or accepted category. Presented were 20th-century paintings and sculpture created by artists with unique visions—many outside of the accepted mainstream for even 20th-century works.

There is yet another thread in the fabric of 20th-century folk expression. Many of the most appreciated artists today are memory painters, such as Grandma Moses and Mattie Lou O'Kelley. Though their pictures are often criticized for purposely nostalgic content, both artists are remarkable for their singular vision, rich palette, and extraordinary sense of composition, which no amount of criticism will diminish. Jane Kallir, in her recent book *Grandma Moses—The Artist Behind the Myth,* illustrates for the first time the fascinating and carefully planned creative efforts of Grandma Moses. Here is a fully developed, 20th-century naive artist producing important art her own way. Her methodology is identical to that used by countless other artists in earlier times.

The legitimacy of 20th-century folk or naive art has been greatly aided by the National Endowment for the Arts, one of the three major federal agencies created to perpetuate the cultural life of America. It recently established a folk arts division, which provides funds for research, film, and exhibitions often featuring the work of living artists. The agency, however, has been dominated by folklorists and folk culturists who, in their zeal for the "folk," occasionally ignore the "art" part of the term. So few cultural and social artifacts constitute art that it becomes imperative to separate the cultural artifact from the folk art object.

Robert T. Teske, folk arts specialist at the National Endowment for the Arts, recently challenged the conservative museum community and its network of supporting collectors in the article "What Is Folk Art" published in *El Palacio,* the Winter 1982–1983 issue of the magazine of the Museum of New Mexico. In many ways his attempts to impose a rigid definition for the term *folk art* were not trailblazing, as I suspect he intended. His ideas merely hark back to the academic traditions of the 1930s and 1940s when only those works created within and by members of a close-knit ethnic or cultural society—such as the Germans in the 18th and 19th centuries in Pennsylvania or the Dutch in the 17th and 18th centuries in the Hudson River Valley—were considered valid. He illustrates his article with several photographs, two of which should be mentioned. The first is a portrait of a mother and child by Ammi Phillips. This painting, by one of the acknowledged folk masters, is not folk art in his opinion. The second illustrates three members of a Michigan family who carry on a family-based wood-carving tradition and produce insignificant carved cedar fans. These he views as a prime example of folk art. I see this restrictive use of the term folk art as unfortunate, a position I believe I share with the distinguished folk art historian Louis C. Jones, who wrote in "The Triumph of American Folk Art" in *Three Eyes on the Past,* "The fact is . . . that a body of paintings, carvings, needle work, and metal work exists which is not part of the fine arts tradition (although sometimes it has been influenced by it). Some of the folk artists were craftsmen with an aesthetic turn of mind. Some were amateurs who learned various skills in secondary school, some were taught professionals. While their work lacks many of the qualities which give us pleasure in the fine arts, it has other qualities which please; a directness of statement, a vigor and originality, a boldness in the use of color, a strong emphasis on rhythm and design.

"Some of what we call American folk art comes from a long handicraft tradition in fairly isolated or restrictive societies: scrimshaw, Pennsylvania German and Swiss religious watercolors known as fraktur, quilts, Hispanic Santos, gravestones, small wooden carvings, the early hand-fashioned trade signs, weathervanes and ship carvings. There is a general agreement that under any definition this is folk art.

"Problems arise, however, over such items as factory-made weathervanes, trade signs which come off an assembly line (e.g., the later wooden Indian), school-taught arts such as theorems, memorials, calligraphy, landscapes after prints, and portraits which show an acquaintance with academic portraiture, all of which have been called folk art for fifty years. The fact is that neither dealers, nor museums, nor collectors, nor magazine writers, nor the general public have made the distinction between the two groups. They have lumped it all together and have called it American folk art. And it is too late I think to change."

It seems to me that the ideas expressed by the well-known collectors and scholars quoted above have merit. Certainly during the entire Colonial period inherited European cultural traditions and decorative motifs continued to influence the artistic efforts of settlers in the New World. I find the notion that only such expressions are valid folk art too restricting, however. This idea would simply deny the so obvious rise of enthusiasm on the part of the immigrant for his newly adopted home and country. Out of this enthusiasm came an extraordinary number of important paintings, sculptures, textiles, ceramics, and metal works which in their own way are a hymn to the American experience.

It is demonstrable that soon after the American Revolution, European traditions gradually began to fade and were replaced by an ever-increasing American consciousness and artistic sensibility. How else can one explain the countless naive artists who even until this day view George Washington as an appropriate subject for paintings and sculpture, the eagle as a symbol for national reverence, and the American flag as an artistic motif of power and beauty. It seems to me that the Americanization of the European folk immigrant led to a truly American folk art—a folk art that continued in nearly every part of the United States in the 20th century.

Be certain, however, not every artist who works in the folk tradition today is a true folk artist. The neo-naives, radial naives, and conscious artists who make folk-inspired art for the marketplace because it is popular and sells should be judged for what they are and for what they create.

However one wishes to view the field and whatever one chooses to label folk art, *American Folk Art of the Twentieth Century* expands our knowledge of the naive artist in 20th-century America. Unlike some others, the authors have felt no need to read into the works abstract theories about the nature of "art." They simply let the painting and sculpture speak for itself. And that it does— quite eloquently. Some collectors may not find their favorites among the artists included here, but that is inevitable. Today, literally hundreds of people have a serious claim to the role of folk artist. All could, of course, not be included in a single volume. However, the authors have wisely balanced recognized earlier figures against rising stars of the present generation to offer the reader the full flavor of the exciting world that is 20th-century American folk art.

This book, with its hundreds of beautiful illustrations and in-depth artist biographies, will find a well-deserved place on the bookshelves of all of those who care about America's rich folk heritage.

Dr. Robert Bishop

# AMERICAN FOLK ART
## OF THE TWENTIETH CENTURY

# Jesse Aaron

The folk sculptor Jesse Aaron was born in Lake City, Florida, in 1887 and lived his entire life in that state. Of mixed white, black, and Seminole Indian ancestry, he was one of eleven children and had to leave school when he was in the second grade to help support his family. After working as a farm laborer, baker, and cook, Aaron found himself without employment—in his middle seventies—when he was forced to sell his flower-and-vegetable nursery in order to pay for a cataract operation for his wife.

Having never been without work, and being a man of strong religious faith, Aaron prayed for guidance. As he described it, his prayers were answered:

> In nineteen sixty-eight, three o'clock in the morning, July the fifth, the Spirit woke me up and said, "Carve wood," one time. I got up three o'clock in the morning, got me a box of oak wood and went to work on it. The next day or two I finished it.

Thus began a career that was to span more than a decade, terminating only with the artist's death in Gainesville, Florida, in 1979.

Aaron's sculpture is strongly anthropomorphic. His carved figures seem to grow out of the very wood itself, something that Aaron hinted at when he declared, "God put the faces in the wood." He chose pieces of cedar or cypress that suggested to him human or animal shapes and worked with them to draw out these forms. Found objects are very much a part of his art. A deer horn may be applied to a piece to suggest an arm or a hand, or bits of clothing, metal, or plastic may be added. Although Aaron did not paint the finished pieces, he scarred many of them with a hot iron to alter their color or texture.

Aaron's techniques were simple and direct. He roughed out forms with a chain saw and finished pieces with chisels, knives, and drills.

Sculpture by Jesse Aaron can be found in various collections. It has been exhibited at the University Gallery, Florida University, Gainesville; the Florida School of Arts, Palatka; and the Tallahassee Junior Museum of Tallahassee, Florida. In 1975, the sculptor was the recipient of a Visual Arts Fellowship from the National Endowment for the Arts.

Jesse Aaron
*Horse's Head*
1970
Carved cedar log; 36″ x 10″
Private collection
Photo by D. James Dee

# J. R. Adkins

The folk painter J. R. Adkins was born in 1907 in York County, South Carolina, and died in Seffner, Florida, in 1973. A hard worker and a bit of a wanderer, Adkins spent his working years traveling around the United States, both as a member of the U.S. Army and as a road-construction crewman. When he was forced into retirement by arthritis in 1969, Adkins, who had been painting for many years, began to paint full-time.

Adkins worked primarily in oils on board or canvas and took as his subject matter both historical topics and humorous incidents, such as the one illustrated in *All Tangled Up,* in which a young woman entangled in a barbed-wire fence stares apprehensively at a nearby bull. In sharp contrast is the drama of a historical work, such as *When Atlanta Burned,* in which the stricken city is seen engulfed in a wall of dancing flames that feed on its buildings like hungry mouths.

Such variation in subject matter reflected not only Adkins's preferences but also his desire to please an audience. As he once remarked:

J. R. Adkins
*All Tangled Up*
1963
Oil on canvas; 24″ x 28″
Collection of Mr. and Mrs. Elias Getz

J. R. Adkins
*When Atlanta Burned*
1965
Oil on canvas; 36″ x 41″
Collection of Mr. and Mrs.
Elias Getz

I've taught myself all that I know about painting. I like to paint things that happened in the past. Civil War, Revolutionary War, Tom Sawyer, Daniel Boone, Kit Carson, Jim Bridger, western landscapes, not just one thing but a combination which gives a variety of subjects. That way you have something that everybody will like.

Paintings by J. R. Adkins are in various collections and have been exhibited at the Museum of American Folk Art, New York City.

# Sylvia Alberts

Born in New York City in 1928 of Russian parents, Sylvia Alberts spends her winters in Manhattan and her summers on a remote island off the coast of Maine. Her paintings are distinguished by brilliant, jewellike colors and an amazing attention to detail. For example, in her *Still Life with Bread Box*, the pale-gray tablecloth is worked with an intricate check pattern that is repeated and shaded just as it would be in the actual covering; pears colored a startling red are superimposed on the flat plane of the golden-yellow tabletop.

Alberts is one of the few 20th-century folk artists who are interested in still lifes, and hers are extraordinarily vital. Like almost all her work, they are done either from photographs or from life. Unlike many folk artists, Alberts never works from memory. She also does portraits, and these, too, are usually fashioned after old photographs, particularly those dating to the period 1930 to 1940. An interesting example is a study based on a snapshot of the entrants in the Miss America pageant of 1945.

Alberts usually works in oil on canvas or Masonite and only rarely in ink on paper. Her painting schedule is extremely regular: nine-to-five, five days a week, sometimes seven days a week in the summer. She rarely works at night and has been painting full-time since 1966.

Sylvia Alberts's works have been exhibited at, among other places, the Washington Gallery of Art, Washington, D.C.; the Reid Gallery, Nashville, Tennessee; the Stephen Gemberling Gallery and Jay Johnson America's Folk Heritage Gallery, both in New York City; and the Boothbay Harbor Region Art Foundation in Maine.

Sylvia Alberts
*Still Life with Bread Box*
1979
Oil on canvas; 30″ x 40″
Baeder/Vogel Collection

Sylvia Alberts
*Class of '49*
1981
Oil on canvas; 16″ x 20″
Collection of Robert and Diane Roskind

*Opposite:* Sylvia Alberts
*Four Generations*
1979
Oil on canvas; 30″ x 36″
Private collection

# Fred K. Alten

The persistent impression of the folk artist as an isolated individual unrecognized by his fellow men is frequently inaccurate. However, this description can be quite accurately applied to Fred K. Alten. Born in Lancaster, Ohio, in 1872, Alten worked for a while for a brother who ran a machine shop in that city, but by 1921 he was in Wyandotte, Michigan, where he worked variously as a laborer, piano mover, carpenter, and foreman at the Ford Motor Company. He remained in Wyandotte until 1943, when, in poor health, he returned to Lancaster. He died there two years later.

Alten's public life was that of an ordinary workingman. But he led a secret life, too. For decades, every night after work, he retired to a small workshop behind his house and painstakingly carved representations of a remarkable variety of both present-day and prehistoric animals. The guide for his labors was an 1880 book entitled *Johnson's Household Book of Nature.* The book illustrated the works of John James Audubon and other well-known 19th-century naturalists. Carved in lifelike poses and painted in rich, natural colors, Alten's creatures began to fill the shelves of the tiny workshop. By the time he stopped working, there were over one

Fred K. Alten
*Carnivora*
ca. 1925
Carved and painted wood;
6″ to 9″ long
Various private collections

Fred K. Alten
*Fighting Dinosaurs*
ca. 1925
Carved and painted wood;
24″ x 15″
The Hall Collection of
American Folk and Isolate
Art

hundred fifty of them, many carefully sealed within wooden cages just as they would appear in a menagerie. Amazingly, it does not appear that Alten ever showed these pieces during his lifetime, and when he left Wyandotte, they were sealed up in the shed. They remained there for thirty years, until they were discovered by collectors and brought to the attention of the art world.

Alten's work was executed with simple carving tools, such as a penknife, but he combined a love of detail (even attempting to duplicate surface texture, such as hair and feathers) with an artist's eye, stylizing his pieces and eliminating unnecessary details.

The works of Fred K. Alten have been exhibited at the Kresge Art Center Gallery, East Lansing, Michigan, as part of the exhibition *Michigan Folk Art: Its Beginnings to 1941*; at the Ella Sharp Museum in Jackson, Michigan; and at the Nassau County Fine Arts Museum, Roslyn, New York.

# Felipe Archuleta

Born in the Sangre de Cristo Mountains of New Mexico in 1910, the Spanish-American carver Felipe Archuleta is heir to the ancient Spanish tradition of *bulto* making, the shaping of wooden religious figures used in churches and home shrines. Like his forefathers, Archuleta works in wood—elm or cottonwood—which he shapes and joins, often employing wood filler to provide more body. Details, such as ears, teeth, and hair, are sometimes made from metal or plastic. The completed figure is covered with gesso and then painted.

Unlike the *santeros,* or "makers of saints," whose work prefigured his, Archuleta does not usually carve religious figures. His interest is primarily in animals, and he has produced dozens of them, ranging from small pigs and cats to giant apes, giraffes, and cougars.

Archuleta's animals are not literal renditions: they are embodiments of the untamed qualities of the animal world. Some are clearly harmless; others are less so; and in all of them there is a feeling of the elemental—the "essential" bear or tiger, whose primordial nature lurks just below the surface.

Archuleta has spent his life in the southwestern United States, working at a variety of trades, including field hand, cook, traveling salesman, and carpenter. It was while he was employed as a carpenter that, in 1967, he found that work was becoming scarce and prayed for a new vocation. Within three days he had picked up "a cheap knife and a cheap rasp" and launched himself on a new career. Today, the backyard of his small adobe house in Tesuque, New Mexico, is filled with figures under construction, and he has found it necessary to employ assistants to help him wrestle with the logistics of meeting incoming orders for his work. This may be a bit more than the carver bargained for, as he has been known to claim that he creates only "to make a living, to buy groceries, to pay bills." However, the life and force of his work speaks to something more than economic necessity.

Sculpture by Felipe Archuleta has been exhibited at the Brooklyn Museum, New York; the Otis Art Institute, Los Angeles, California; and the Museum of International Folk Art, Santa Fe, New Mexico.

Felipe Archuleta
*Koala Bear*
1976
Carved and assembled wood painted with applied details of
excelsior, plastic, and metal; 26″ x 23″
The Hall Collection of American Folk and Isolate Art

Felipe Archuleta
*Lynx*
1975
Carved and assembled wood painted with applied details of
excelsior and plastic; 36″ x 15″
The Hall Collection of American Folk and Isolate Art

# Eddie Arning

The difficult life of Eddie Arning has spawned a strange and powerful art. Born in 1898 near Kenney, Texas, of German immigrant parents, Arning was committed to a state mental institution in his teens for reasons no one seems to remember. Nearly his entire life was spent behind the walls of the institution: he was not released until he was seventy-eight years old. Sometime during the last decade of his confinement, Arning began to draw on paper with wax crayons like those schoolchildren use. His efforts attracted attention, and eventually he was provided with professional oil-base crayons and high-quality paper.

Arning's work developed from initial interpretations of single objects, usually in strong colors, to more complex, though always highly schematic and individualized, compositions. His first efforts seem to have been inspired by childhood recollections of his family and farm life. Later on, he was influenced by the pictures and advertisements he saw in magazines and newspapers. Completely innocent of any knowledge of the rules of painting and desiring only to, in his words, make "a nice picture," Arning gradually developed a style that was both interpretative and symbolic. Certain stances—the raised arm, the Egyptian-like profile—occur over and over, and when combined with the use of strong colors in flat planes, they create a compelling, ritualistic structure. Arning's paintings seem to have little to do with our world—even when the overall composition is based on a picture or a memory of that world.

Tragically, when Arning was released from the mental institution, he seemed to lose the drive and inspiration that had fueled his work. Faced with a larger outside world, his own creative world slowly faded away.

Paintings by Eddie Arning have been exhibited at, among other places, the Museum of International Folk Art, Santa Fe, New Mexico; the Museum of American Folk Art, New York City; the Museum of Art, Columbus, Georgia; and the Renaissance Society at the University of Chicago.

Eddie Arning
*Camping*
1960–70
Pastel and crayon on paper; 19″ x 25″
Collection of Rubens Teles
Photo by Bill Buckner

Eddie Arning
*Untitled*
ca. 1970
Crayon and pastel on paper;
19″ x 25″
Private collection
Photo by Bill Buckner

# Steve Ashby

Although he lived his entire life in Fauquier County, Virginia, a region near Washington, D.C., that is home to some of the richest and most sophisticated people in the world, Steve Ashby's work reflected an entirely different way of life —that of the rural folk sculptor. Born in 1904 in the tiny village of Delaplane, where he remained until his death in 1980, Ashby was a farm hand, sometime hotel waiter, and gardener until his retirement in the early 1960s. It seems that he was always a carver, but he began to work at carving seriously only after the death of his wife in 1962.

Ashby's work falls into two general categories. In the first category are small figures made from saw-cut plywood that are painted, always with model-airplane paints, and frequently embellished with various found objects, such as plastic rings, metal pop-bottle tops—whatever Ashby had on hand. Many of these small pieces have faces that Ashby created by gluing a picture cut from a magazine onto the shaped head. Some of the smaller pieces are hinged or mounted on swivels so that they can move in the wind in the manner of whirligigs.

In the second category are large, almost life-size humans and animals carved from tree trunks and branches that Ashby gathered in nearby woods. After his wife's death, these large figures became Ashby's "family," and he often not only painted them but also meticulously dressed them, sometimes in his wife's old clothing. He adorned some of them with costume jewelry, old hats, and even shoes.

The sculpture and assemblages that Ashby made reflected his past and his reworking of memory material. Much of his inspiration came to him in dreams. The urgency of this creative force is revealed in a remark he once made about a piece he had just finished: "I knew I could do it. . . . I kept thinking about it. I dreamed about it. I just had to do it."

The subjects of Ashby's work vary. Some examples, such as *Man with Scythe* (a self-portrait reflecting the sculptor's fondness for field work), are related to rural life. Others, including some pornographic examples that display complete anatomical detail, reveal his exposure to "girlie-book" literature. Whatever the subject matter, Ashby brought to it a unique and individual consciousness.

Examples of sculpture by Steve Ashby can be found in various collections. Among the exhibitions in which they have appeared is *Six Naives*, mounted in 1973 by the Akron Art Institute, Akron, Ohio.

Steve Ashby
*Receiving a Package*
ca. 1970
Carved and painted wood; 18″ x 20″ x 7″
Collection of Chuck and Jan Rosenak
Photo by Joel Breger

*Opposite:* Steve Ashby
*Girl in Bikini*
ca. 1970
Carved and painted wood;
9½″ x 6¾″ x ¾″
Collection of Chuck and Jan
Rosenak
Photo by Joel Breger

# Joseph P. Aulisio

The folk painter Joseph P. Aulisio was born in 1910 at Old Forge, Pennsylvania, a town with about 9,000 inhabitants located not far from Scranton in northeastern Pennsylvania. He appears to have spent most of his life in the Scranton area, where he worked in a laundry and dry-cleaning establishment. Appropriately enough, one of Aulisio's best-known works, *Portrait of Frank Peters, the Tailor*, done in 1965, memorializes a fellow worker in the cleaning and tailoring business.

Like many other folk artists, Aulisio did not begin to paint until late in life. As he once remarked, "I always dreamed of becoming an artist and writer, but early years were too busy earning a living." In his fifties, Aulisio established himself as a painter after being greatly encouraged by the acceptance of his work at a local museum. Though he declared, "I paint because I love it," he also noted that, "Winning a top prize in a regional show at Everhart Museum in Scranton encouraged me to paint more." Aulisio's work is primarily oils on canvas and is highlighted by deeply sensitive portraits in which the character of the model is carefully developed. There is great attention to detail and a skillful use of balanced colors.

The paintings of Joseph Aulisio are in various public and private collections, including that of the Museum of American Folk Art in New York City and the Everhart Museum, Scranton, Pennsylvania. His work has also been widely exhibited throughout the eastern United States.

Joseph P. Aulisio
*Portrait of Frank Peters, the Tailor*
1965
Oil on canvas; 28″ x 20″
Museum of American Folk Art

# Calvin and Ruby Black

A few piles of rubble in the California desert near Yermo are all that remain of one of the most remarkable examples of conceptual folk art ever assembled. The creators, Calvin and Ruby Black, were born in the South (Calvin in Tennessee, Ruby in Georgia). They married in 1933 and lived most of their lives in northern California. In 1953, they bought—sight unseen—a plot of land near Yermo and opened a rock shop. After a new road brought an influx of travelers, the Blacks began to create a miniature amusement park which they called Possum Trot. Among the attractions were wind-driven constructions, merry-go-rounds, a train, and several stagecoaches, but the heart of the exhibition was the Bird Cage Theater and its "fantasy doll show," a mixture of stage show and vaudeville act performed by some seventy carved and painted dolls.

Numerous paintings, totems, and signs were salvaged from Possum Trot after Ruby's death in 1980, but the most important pieces are the dolls. Averaging three to four feet in height, they were carved and painted by Calvin and dressed, usually in scraps of old clothing, by Ruby. Almost everything in the Possum Trot assemblage came from a local dump. After Calvin's death in 1972, a friend noted, "Everything that man had he built. He never bought nothin'."

Today, the dolls are in collections scattered throughout the United States, but they were originally intended to be seen together as the characters in the various Bird Cage Theater productions. Calvin, an old-time carnival and circus man, wrote the songs, music, and dialogue used in these performances. He recorded the sound and played it back through tape recorders placed in the heads of some of the figures. The environment thus created was totally dependent on Calvin, and the buildings and figures fell into disuse when he died.

The dolls made by Calvin and Ruby Black have a powerful totemic quality. The heads of the dolls are their most important feature, for their bodies are often little more than armatures on which the costumes were hung. The hair on some of the early examples was carved; Calvin later used human wigs. Although their creators thought of them as quite "human," the dolls have an abstracted, otherworldly quality that goes beyond human experience.

Possum Trot was the subject of a 1974 documentary movie, *Possum Trot: The Life and Work of Calvin Black,* and the dolls have been exhibited at, among other places, the Museum of American Folk Art in New York City and the Mojave River Valley Museum in Barstow, California.

Calvin and Ruby Black
*Lula Bell*
1953–66
Carved and painted wood with applied cloth costume and radio speaker mounted in head; 24″ x 7″
The Hall Collection of American Folk and Isolate Art

Calvin and Ruby Black
*Miss Paulette*
1953–66
Carved and painted wood, fabric, and metal; 35″ high
Collection of Mr. Jon Reyes

# Dewey Douglas Blocksma

The remarkable constructions of Dewey Douglas Blocksma can be traced directly to his background as a physician. Born in Amarillo, Texas, in 1943, Blocksma attended medical school and found himself particularly intrigued by anatomy. This interest was a continuation of his lifelong curiosity about "how things worked."

Blocksma spent six years working as a doctor in hospital emergency rooms, a scarifying and horrifying experience. During this period, he began to construct figures, or "toys," as he calls them, both as a form of amusement and as an emotional safety valve from the constant tensions of life-and-death situations.

Blocksma eventually found that two things were coming to dominate his time and thought: his figures and house construction, or, rather, reconstruction, since he likes to take houses apart and put them back together. In 1979, he left medicine to devote himself full-time to these pursuits.

Blocksma now lives in a small frame house in Holland, Michigan, surrounded by pieces of his constructions. These strange, anthropoid figures, which resemble dolls or even whirligigs, are made from bits of junk—wood, leather, piano wire, canvas, and odd bits of hardware—jointed together so that their arms and legs move. There is a casual, almost accidental quality to the work, but the thought behind it is far from accidental. It is, in fact, highly premeditated. As the artist says, "I use the works to think about things I am trying to understand."

This search for understanding has led Blocksma to study the relationships among the materials with which he constructs a piece—"trying to let each material say itself in a construction. Many voices taking turns or not"—and to express through his work the conversations, cries for help, touches of humor and pathos that haunt him from his emergency-room days. For Blocksma, the constructions become a form of exorcism of personal devils.

Dewey Blocksma's work has been included in exhibitions at the Mulvane Art Center in Topeka, Kansas, and at the Silvermine Guild Center for the Arts, New Canaan, Connecticut, where it was part of the *Folk, Fantasy & Expressionism* exhibition. His work has also been shown at the Watergate Building, Washington, D.C.

Dewey Douglas Blocksma
*Under the Windmill*
1982
Mixed media; 31″ x 19″
Jay Johnson America's Folk
Heritage Gallery

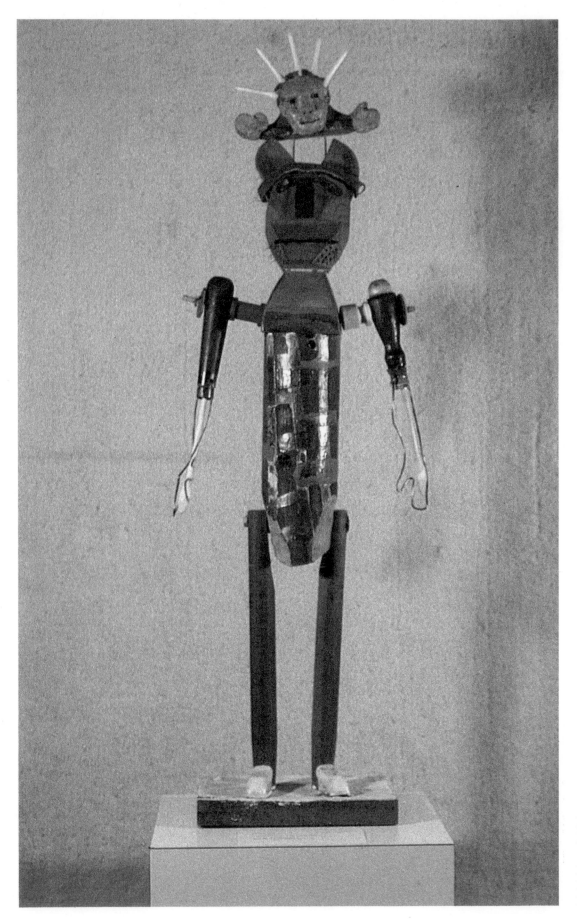

Dewey Douglas Blocksma
*Both Sides of the Brain*
1982
Mixed media; 33″ high
Private collection
Photo by Bill Buckner

# Peter "Charlie" Bochero

Peter "Charlie" Bochero—famous as simply Peter Charlie—has an important place among those artists who cut themselves off from the world and, in lonely isolation, hide their work from the public while creating fantastic universes that express their hopes and fears. Born in Armenia, Charlie migrated to this country in 1903. He settled on a farm in rural Leechburg, Pennsylvania, and except for a brief trip back to Armenia to fight for his homeland during World War I, he spent the rest of his life in that state. He died in 1962.

Other than the few contacts necessitated by his work, Charlie shunned human companionship and lived as a hermit. Few people had any idea of how he passed his leisure hours. It was only after his death in 1962 that the opening of a garage he had rented behind the local hardware store revealed a treasure trove of paintings, some seventy in all. Peter Charlie was a folk painter, and a remarkably good one.

One can find various influences in Charlie's work: religious beliefs, Armenian folk motifs, dramatic moments in American history, and, perhaps most important, a fascination with space, demons, and elements that seem almost to be dredged up from the unconscious. All the many components are blended together in Charlie's paintings. For example, in *Crucifixion,* a despairing Christ raises his eyes to a huge spaceship that sweeps into the picture from the left while an Indian tends a campfire below; the periphery is dominated by a demonic eye, an octopus, and various earthly and unearthly beings. The meaning of this cosmology is lost to us, but its power is unquestioned, as are the remarkable directness of the artist's vision and his unusual composition. In one untitled painting, figures of men, gods, and planetary visitors float in universal embrace against a tapestrylike background of stars and planets. The effect is that of a Persian miniature or a Rajput painting, but it is doubtful that Charlie ever had any familiarity with either. Although some of his paintings are oils on canvas, the majority are executed in house paints, sometimes with sand mixed in to provide a textured surface.

Peter Charlie's work has been exhibited at various galleries, including that of Phyllis Kind in New York City and the Farmhouse Gallery in Inkster, Michigan. It is also in various public and private collections.

Peter "Charlie" Bochero
*Untitled*
ca. 1959
Oil on canvas; 24″ x 36″
Epstein/Powell American Primitives
Photo by Bill Buckner

Peter "Charlie" Bochero
*Untitled*
ca. 1959
Oil on canvas; 24″ x 36″
Epstein/Powell American Primitives

# Milton Bond

Milton Bond is one of the very few folk artists working in the exacting medium of reverse-glass painting. Born in New York City in 1918, Bond began to draw at the age of five, but an active life as a New England sailor and oysterman prevented him from devoting much time to his art. For years, he was the master of one of the last commercial sailing ships operating out of Long Island, and his trips up and down the coast of New England and in and out of New York harbor offered a wealth of experience and visual memories.

About twenty years ago, Bond began to set these visions down, but he did not do so on canvas or wood or paper, as is the case with most folk artists. Instead, he turned to reverse-glass painting, an ancient art practiced in both Europe and America. The painting is done in oils on the back of a piece of clear glass. The glass protects the painting. The painting must be done in reverse of the usual order, the tiny frontal details put in first and the background last. It is very demanding work, but Bond mastered this difficult technique without any professional help. The small size of his works make his art even more remarkable.

Bond's paintings, bucolic rural scenes and busy urban vistas churning with activity, are suffused with a strange background light achieved by the effective use of oils on the transparent surface. The foregrounds of his paintings are filled with the kind of details of which folk artists are so fond: engineers can be glimpsed in the cabs of tiny locomotives; specks of mother-of-pearl attached to the glass (a technique well known to earlier reverse-glass painters) cause the many windows of a city office building to glow with the colors of a setting sun.

Milton Bond's work is in several major collections, including those of the Grand Palais in Paris and the Hartford, Connecticut, Atheneum. They have been exhibited not only in the United States but also in Germany, Switzerland, and France. He was the winner of the 1982 silver medal at the Swiss International Folk Art exhibition. He now lives and works in Fairfield, Connecticut.

Milton Bond
*Brooklyn Bridge, 1924*
1981
Reverse painting on glass;
16" x 20"
Collection of Laura Sullivan
Photo by Bill Buckner

Milton Bond
*New York, N.Y., 1923*
1982
Reverse painting on glass;
20″ x 28″
Private collection

Milton Bond
*Blue Depot, Winter*
1981
Reverse painting on glass;
8″ x 10″
Jay Johnson America's Folk
Heritage Gallery

# Mary Borkowski

A textile artist in the tradition of the 18th- and 19th-century women who created samplers, needlework pictures, and Berlin work, Mary Borkowski works in silk thread on a felt or velvet background. Her compositions are based on bits of her own life, but they assume a surreal quality as she reworks them. As she notes:

> They are the pieces of my life that shouldn't have been—the world of Mary Borkowski. I always feel safe when applying thread with my hands. I feel my hands are a second brain, just automatically pushing a needle around. These paintings done with needle, thread and cloth are expressions of awful truths and deep emotional experiences of self, of others, and God's creations.

The inner convictions that fuel Borkowski's work often seem almost too powerful for the medium. Searing psychological insights, such as the hauteur and loneliness of *Next to Me You Are Nothing* (a study of a dowdy woman sitting on a park bench flanked by "others," whose bodies are only suggested by outline stitching), and outcries against social and economic injustice like *The Crash* strain the fabric on which they are worked.

Borkowski does not see her "string pictures," as she calls them, as a form of embroidery. Indeed, she points out that she builds up her designs in thread as one might form a clay pot or paint a picture. They have a distinct texture and a feeling of being "constructed" rather than stitched.

Mary Borkowski was born in 1916 in Sulphur Springs, Ohio, and now lives in Dayton. She made her first string picture in 1965 as a memorial to a close friend and since then has found her life to be closely occupied with her art. Her work can be found in various public and private collections and has been exhibited at the Museum of International Folk Art, Santa Fe, New Mexico, and at the White House, Washington, D.C.

*Following page:*
Mary Borkowski
*The Slap*
1974
Silk, wool, lace, and thread;
20¼" x 15"
Collection of Mr. and Mrs.
Elias Getz

# Emile Branchard

Like their academic counterparts, folk artists often have distinct preferences as to subject matter. The painter Emile Branchard always preferred landscapes and rarely included people in his paintings. His stark paintings often rely for their effect on the sharp contrast between a muted background and much lighter frontal elements. For example, in *Trees and Rocks,* a clump of dead white birch seems to leap out of the dark greens and browns of a pine grove. Although he preferred nature, Branchard dealt with it secondhand, as a memory painter, rather than working from a scene before him. He noted that, for him, "Nature runs faster than you can catch her."

Born in New York City in 1881, Branchard held a variety of jobs—truck driver, civilian-defense policeman—and took in boarders to help make ends meet. It was, in fact, one of his roomers who launched Branchard on his career. An artist who was unable to pay his rent left paints and canvas to cover the bill, and Branchard used them to do his first work. The first impression stuck, for he always preferred to work in oils on canvas.

After a siege of tuberculosis forced him from the job market, Branchard devoted much of his time to painting, producing a body of interesting work. His philosophy of art was simple and homespun: "Painting is like cooking. You must have the right ingredients and know how to mix them. Colors are like men and women. Some mix and some don't. When they do, it's marriage, and when they don't, it's divorce."

Emile Branchard
*Trees and Rocks*
not dated
Oil on canvas; 20″ x 28″
Collection of Richard and
Suzanne Barancik
Photo by David R. Williams

# David Butler

The octogenarian constructionalist David Butler was born in Saint Mary Parish, Louisiana, in 1898, and now lives at Patterson, a few miles from Morgan City, Louisiana. Though his father was a carpenter, Butler received no art and little craft training. Moreover, he is illiterate. After his retirement from a variety of menial jobs, he began to create remarkable sculptures and whirligigs from discarded bits of tin that he cut, folded, and painted.

Butler is, in the purest sense, an environmentalist: his art is designed to fit into the space in which he lives and to relate to other similar pieces to create a conceptual whole. With Butler, the focus of this art is not his home or workshop or a gallery but the small yard around his house. This he fills with a moving circus of constructions made of cut and painted tin. Some are whirligigs, or wind toys, which turn constantly, presenting a new shape to the viewer with each vagrant gust of wind. Others are stable. The pieces all relate to one another and to the artist's total conception of the moment.

Butler does not confine this activity to his yard. He also has a bicycle, his sole means of transportation, which is decorated with similar creations in tin and plastic—birds, flowers, flags—many of which move as the wheels turn and the wind blows, a graphic example of taking one's art to the viewer. The subject matter of Butler's work is both secular and biblical, but it is always filtered through the artist's particular perception. As he notes, "I see them things at night when I lay down, and I get up and cut them out just like I see it."

Butler traces the outlines of his constructions on pieces of old tin. They are then shaped with tin shears and a meat cleaver. They are painted with house paints—Butler prefers red, yellow, blue, and green, with black and white accents—and embellished with found objects, such as costume jewelry and plastic flowers.

Works by David Butler are in various collections and have been exhibited at, among other places, the New Orleans Museum of Art and the Museum of American Folk Art in New York City.

David Butler
*Alligator*
not dated
Cut-out metal; 37½" long
Collection of Herbert W. Hemphill, Jr.
Photo by Bill Buckner

# Miles Carpenter

Miles Carpenter is one of this century's most important carvers in the folk idiom. For over forty years, his powerful and symbolic representations of humans, animals, and biblical characters have been dominating the galleries and museums in which they are shown. Some of these carved and painted creatures are created from scratch; others, such as his incredible *Hydra-Headed Monster*, are developed from natural objects, such as a gnarled tree root. Carpenter gives each of his works a unique individual touch that makes it distinctive.

Carpenter comes to his craft naturally. Born near Lititz, Pennsylvania, in 1889, he was taken at an early age to Waverly, Virginia, where his father established a sawmill. By 1912, Carpenter was running his own mill. He continued to run the mill, off and on, until he retired in 1957. It was during a lull in this business that he began to carve. He describes his career since that time in succinct terms:

> Somehow, in nineteen forty, the lumber business got dull, and to keep doing something I started carving, mostly animals. A year or two later, I quit carving until I retired in nineteen fifty-seven. I could not sit down and do nothing, so I went back to carving again. In nineteen sixty-six, I lost my dear wife and things seemed real dull. However, I kept on carving and am at it now. I love to make things out of wood.

Carpenter's work often has an apocalyptic quality. A snarling devil holds the sinner above the boiling pits of hell in *The Devil and the Damned*. The viewer is threatened by the gaping jaws and ragged teeth of the hydra; everything stands poised on the brink of the abyss. The impending doom and terror create a tension

Miles Carpenter
*Frog*
1978
Carved and painted wood;
15″ long
Private collection
Photo by Bill Buckner

Miles Carpenter
*Woman and Greyhound*
1971
Carved and painted wood;
19″ x 19½″
The Hall Collection of
American Folk and Isolate
Art

uncharacteristic of most folk art that is immediately appealing to the sophisticated viewer. Works by Carpenter were included in the exhibit *Transmitters: The Isolate Artist in America,* organized by the Philadelphia College of Art in 1981, and have been shown at numerous galleries and museums, including the Abby Aldrich Rockefeller Folk Art Center, Williamsburg, Virginia.

# Bob Carter

Born in Turley, Oklahoma, in 1928, Bobby Eugene Carter went west with an older brother during the Great Depression and established himself in the California mountains, where he worked for many years as a logger. The loneliness caused by the early deaths of his parents was increased by the long months of relative solitude in the rough logging camps, where the deer, birds, and small woodland animals were often more numerous than humans. Though he eventually married, settled in Oroville, California, and raised a family, Carter never forgot the mountains. At the age of forty-five, with no previous training in the arts, he began to set down on canvas his memories of those days in the lumber camps, of fishing and hunting trips, and of the grandeur and isolation of the great Sierra.

Carter works in acrylics on Masonite and takes as his subject matter scenes of activity: men working in the woods, trucks hauling out the enormous logs, all the hustle and bustle of a woodsman's life. He also paints quiet interiors: a woman preparing breakfast for her husband or children playing. Regardless of subject, Carter handles the paints to create textures reminiscent of the woods. Patches of bare ground, walls, floors, even a shirt remind one of the rough bark of a tree or the striated surface of a freshly cut pine log.

Though he now has a "nine-to-five" job as yard supervisor for a lumber company, Carter still follows the ways of the woods in his painting. He rises early, sometimes at three or four in the morning—"when it's quiet and peaceful," he says —and goes to work, and when his inspiration lags, he drives back in the mountains, where the sights and sounds evoke memories of the past.

Carter's work has been exhibited at various museums, including Piece Hall Gallery, the Woodspring Museum, and the University of East Anglia—all in England —and, in 1975, he received the bronze medal at the California State Fair for his painting *Mill Town*.

Bob Carter
*Logging Truck*
1978
Oil on Masonite; 24″ x 48″
Private collection

Bob Carter
*Logger Kitchen*
1979
Oil on Masonite; 18″ x 16½″
Collection of Peter Muccio
Photo by D. James Dee

# William Ned Cartledge

Unlike the great majority of folk artists, William Ned Cartledge uses his works to express his opinions of world events. The sharp social commentary evident in much of Cartledge's art reflects his convictions, giving his carvings both intellectual and aesthetic importance.

Born in Cannon, Georgia, in 1916, and now a resident of Atlanta, Cartledge was employed for decades in the cotton trade and then worked as a salesman for a Sears Roebuck store until his retirement in 1982. He always devoted his spare time in the evenings to carving. When he was growing up in small-town Georgia, most young boys carried a pocketknife, and whittling was an accepted way to pass the time for young and old alike. Although Cartledge carved such things as guns and knives, he lost interest in the craft as he grew older, and it was not until late in life that the purchase of a set of X-Acto knives rekindled his love for wood carving. At first he made simple boxes, but in time he developed complex carvings in relief on pine, poplar, and basswood.

Set within frames and painted in acrylics (he painted a few early works in oils), these relief-carved works reflect their creator's strongly held social and political views. In *Garden of Eden,* a disgruntled Adam and Eve are driven forth, Coke bottles in hand, from a paradise that comes equipped with a television set—the "rabbit ears" of which are those of a real rabbit (a bit of the quirky humor that permeates much of Cartledge's work)—and which is surrounded by an all-too-neat white picket fence. The white fence as a social and racial symbol emerges again in *White Fence,* in which black hands set against a background of red and orange flames grasp the pickets as though they were prison bars.

Working slowly and carefully painting his finished pieces with acrylics, Cartledge produces no more than five or six works each year, and he has been inactive for considerable periods. As a consequence, the number of his works is small. Even so, he is highly regarded, and his compositions are found in the collections of the High Museum of Art, Atlanta, Georgia, and the Lyndon Baines Johnson Library and Museum of Austin, Texas, as well as in various important private collections.

William Ned Cartledge
*Garden of Eden*
1979
Relief-carved wood painted
with acrylic; 23″ x 16½″
Private collection

William Ned Cartledge
*Communist Loaf*
1979
Relief-carved wood painted
with acrylic; 20″ x 24″
Collection of the artist

# Bill Chute

The folk painter Bill Chute was fascinated with the sights and sounds of America's railways from an early age and has devoted himself to recreating on canvas the "iron horses" of yesteryear. In few artists are art and biography so closely interwoven. Chute was born in Brooklyn, in 1929, under the viaduct of the old Fifth Avenue elevated railway. By the age of six, he was regularly traveling alone from Brooklyn to New Rochelle, where he now lives. He always knew that he wanted to do nothing else but work on the railways, and by fifteen he was a track worker for the New York City subway system, graduating from there to the New York–New Haven line.

In 1969, at the age of forty, Chute set out to teach himself to paint. At first he did only portraits, but in 1976 he started depicting on canvas the history of the New York City transit system from 1832 to today. In 1977, he sold twenty of these canvases to the New York City Transit Authority Museum, and his career was launched.

Recognized by the Transit Authority as "the subway artist," Chute has become a chronicler of the subways and trains he remembers so vividly from the 1930s and 1940s. He employs period references to recreate railroad scenes from even earlier eras. All of these works are characterized by an extreme attention to exact detail. Horsecars, trains, and even buildings are painted to duplicate examples that existed during the period portrayed. A model-railroad buff and a keen historian of railway lore, Chute spends much of his time painting and building model trains. He works at home, painting whenever he can. His paintings are in oils on canvas.

Chute has won several awards for his paintings, including the Adolph Grant Award at the New Rochelle, New York, Art Association juried exhibition of 1978. His works have been shown at the Bridge Gallery and the Westlake Gallery, both in White Plains, New York.

Bill Chute
*South Ferry & Brooklyn
Bridge*
1981
Oil on canvas; 20″ x 24″
Collection of Mr. and Mrs.
Michael Donovan
Photo by Bill Buckner

# Clark Coe

The creative impulse that causes a folk artist to begin to work varies with the individual. With some, it is the new freedom that comes with retirement; with others, boredom or the hope of financial gain. With Clark Coe, it was pity. Stricken at the sight of a young bedridden nephew, Coe resolved to provide the child with something to entertain him. It was around 1910, and television was far in the future. Relying on his familiarity with carnival rides and whirligigs, Coe devised and constructed a remarkable environment of some forty carved and painted figures. These humans and animals had articulated joints and were connected to a small waterwheel set in a nearby river. As the water turned the wheel, the animals moved about in a veritable symphony of activity, bringing joy to the shut-in child.

Coe's creation was put out each spring when the river was free of ice and taken in again at "freeze-up" time in the fall. After several years, the family moved away, and the figures were put into storage, where they remained for decades until discovered by an antiques dealer. These remarkably ingenious figures, of which *Girl on a Pig* is a good example, are made of saw-cut and carved wood and often incorporate parts of barrels, bits of metal, ribbon, and horsehair. Their almost totemic features and clever mechanical arrangement make these pieces among the more interesting of 20th-century articulated sculpture. Originally from Killingworth, Connecticut, the pieces are now in various collections. They have been exhibited at the Museum of American Folk Art and were part of the Brooklyn Museum's 1976 exhibition *Folk Sculpture USA*.

Clark Coe
*Girl on a Pig*
ca. 1910
Carved and painted wood,
articulated; 37″ high
Collection of Herbert W.
Hemphill, Jr.

# The Reverend
# Richard P. Cooper

Although he was born in the city of Pittsburgh, the Reverend Richard P. Cooper
has spent most of his life in the Pennsylvania farm country, and the sights and
ways of that land have inspired his work. Born in 1938, Cooper did not begin to
paint until 1975, but he had been interested in art for a long time and comes from
a line of artists, most prominent of whom was a Scottish great grandfather who was
a portrait painter. Unlike many folk artists, Cooper has an acute critical sense that
made him reluctant to paint: because of his education, background, and the fact
that his wife was an art major in college, he was afraid his work would be criticized.

For many years, he served as pastor to two small Lutheran churches and tended
his small farm in Creekside, Pennsylvania, soaking in the sights and sounds of the
countryside. In 1975, working in secret, he produced his first painting: a farm
scene filled with childhood memories. Encouraged by his wife and supported by art
collectors, Cooper has continued to paint. The number of his paintings is small:
Cooper is a part-time painter, working primarily in the early mornings, in the
evenings, and on holidays, snatching whatever time is available from pulpit and plow.

Cooper's early work was done in oils on Masonite; in a few instances he
achieved the effect of a collage by attaching carved wooden figures to the painted
surface. In recent years he has worked in oils on canvas, sometimes also employing
acrylics on wood or Masonite as well as on canvas.

The twin themes of religion and rural life pulsate through Cooper's vibrantly
colored and highly detailed work. Although pastoral, these paintings are never
static or simply "pretty." They are infused with a sense of rural activity. Farmers
rake, sow, and plow; housewives hang out the wash or cook the enormous meals
demanded by such strenuous activity. Even the children are busy, milking cows,
carrying the wash, or feeding the chickens.

In a sense, Cooper is a memory painter, for much of his work is drawn from
childhood experience, but he is always looking for new ideas and new themes. He
carries with him paper and pencil with which he can render quick sketches to be
later turned into more fully developed drawings on pieces of butcher paper the size
of the canvas on which the final painting will be done.

Much more articulate than most folk painters, Cooper defines his work as
dependent on color, design, and emotional content. He enjoys talking about his
work with other people and even serves as "artist in residence" at local grammar
schools.

The works of the Reverend Richard P. Cooper, which are customarily signed

Rev. Richard P. Cooper
*Monday Is Wash Day*
1978
Oil on canvas; 22″ x 28″
Private collection

"Rev. Cooper," are in the permanent collections of the John Judkyn Memorial at Freshford Manor, Bath, England, and Pennsylvania's Johnstown Museum. They have been shown at numerous galleries, including Webb & Parsons, New Canaan, Connecticut; the Bede Gallery of the Central School of Art & Design, London; and the Piece Hall Gallery at Halifax, England.

Rev. Richard P. Cooper
*It's Spring and Time to Work*
1981
Oil on canvas; 22″ x 28″
Jay Johnson America's Folk
Heritage Gallery

# James Crane

James Crane is one of the more important folk painters with a New England background. Though little is known of his early years, it appears that he did not begin to paint until late in life. At that time, he was living near Elsworth, Maine, a small market town not far from Bar Harbor. Few people in that area live far from the sea, and few men fail to have extensive contact with it. Consequently, it is not surprising that most of Crane's few existing works focus on ships or seaport towns.

Crane's interpretations of a ship portrait, such as *The Titanic,* or of a harbor scene, such as *Dream Island,* vary sharply from the usual rendering. Perspective is so wildly skewed that it is possible, for example, to view *The Titanic* from several angles at one time—from the side, looking down on the deck, at an angle, and so forth. This multiplicity of perspectives and lack of a single light source are, of course, characteristics of much primitive painting, but in few cases are they used so dramatically.

Crane painted on a variety of found materials—bedsheet, plywood, canvas, and oilcloth—and he employed both commercial artist oils and common house paint. The tragedy of the *Titanic,* which sank in 1912, seems to have fascinated Crane, for he painted several versions of the ship (many years after it sank). Other works are less literal, combining aspects of the familiar seaport town with fantasy elements. Most of these date to the 1960s, only a few years before the artist's death.

James Crane
*Dream Island*
ca. 1966
House paint on bedsheet
with paper collage; 18½″ x
30″
The Hall Collection of
American Folk and Isolate
Art

# John Cross

The carver John Cross was born in Dover, New Jersey, in 1935, and now resides in New York City. Cross works as an advertising staff writer, and his intricately carved figures reflect the life he leads. Most of Cross's carvings are of groups: businessmen shaking hands at the conclusion of a "deal," a gang of the "good-old boys" playing cards, people walking, conversing, taking part in the many busy activities typical of life in New York City. Cross brings his own particular touch to each of the figures and to their many interrelationships.

The figures are small, twelve to sixteen inches high, and at first glance seem deceptively plain despite the bright colors in which they are painted. They are so sharply modeled, so clearly defined, that the viewer gets a feeling of strength and mass that completely belies the small size of the objects.

The sophistication of Cross's work reflects the fact that he has been perfecting his art over a long period of time. He has whittled for most of his life, and he now whittles wherever he goes. His pieces are composed of various small elements (heads, arms, legs) glued together when finished to create the final figure, and Cross carries his pocketknife (the only tool he ever uses) and the units he is working on in a small bag. While walking, waiting on line, or talking, he takes out his knife and the piece and whittles.

There is a joy and pleasure about Cross's work that reflects his own happy, stable life with his wife and son—winters in a sunny Manhattan apartment, summers in the country. This pleasant stability is very different from the obsession and striving that mark the work of so many other folk artists.

Work by John Cross can be found in the collection of the John Judkyn Memorial, Freshford Manor, Bath, England. It has been exhibited at Webb & Parsons, New Canaan, Connecticut; the Shirley Scott Gallery, Southampton, New York; and in several English museums, including the Piece Hall Gallery, Halifax, and the gallery of the University of East Anglia at Norwich.

John Cross
*Adam and Eve*
1979
Carved and painted wood;
23″ x 12″
Collection of Mr. and Mrs.
Malcolm M. Knapp

John Cross
*Card Players*
1979
Carved and painted wood;
figures are 12″ x 5″; the table
is 6½″ high and 9″ in diame-
ter; the dog is 3″ x 4″
Collection of the artist

John Cross
*Keeping Up with the News*
1980
Carved and painted wood;
14″ high
Collection of Jeanne Neary
Look

# Earl Cunningham

If there is a rule that applies to folk painters and their art, it is that there are no rules. Each artist is unique. Earl Cunningham is a case in point. While most folk artists paint first for pleasure or through compulsion and only later seek to sell their creations, Cunningham sold his first work within a few days of its completion and always regarded his paintings as marketable commodities. This attitude probably reflects the artist's life.

Born in the coastal town of Edgcombe, Maine, in 1893, Cunningham was on his own at an early age, working up and down the Maine coast as a tinker and itinerant salesman of small objects. Since he traded in everything from fish to sewing needles, it was quite natural to him to also sell his paintings. By the age of sixteen, he was using dime-store paints to create land- and seascapes on bits of driftwood salvaged along the coast. Offered at fifty cents apiece, these works, like his later paintings, dealt with the sea, rural farms, and the animals and birds of the shore and forest with which he had become well acquainted during his ramblings.

The artist's horizon expanded as he grew older. He sailed as a crewman on commercial vessels up and down the Atlantic coast, learned how to repair automobiles, and became knowledgeable about rocks and minerals. Between the world wars, he and his wife developed several tourist museums, ran a chicken farm, and sold everything they could sell. They finally settled in St. Augustine, Florida, where for twenty-five years Cunningham ran an antiques shop and acquired a reputation as a cantankerous, unpredictable character. He was sometimes referred to as "the crusty dragon."

Cunningham was perhaps less cantankerous than shrewd. He knew the lure of the unattainable, and in selling both his antiques and his paintings, he always played hard to get. Of the estimated five hundred works he produced, he appears to have sold less than half. Of the remainder, some are unaccounted for, but most were carefully doled out as his reputation grew. Nearly two hundred of his works were shown at a single Daytona exhibition.

Characterized by a bold, crude palette emphasizing broad planes of color and arbitrary spacial relationships, Cunningham's works feature recurring leitmotifs, such as the angel Gabriel and jewellike flowering palm trees. These paintings are sufficiently appealing to have acquired a wide audience.

The paintings of Earl Cunningham are in the permanent collections of the family of the late John Kennedy and the Michigan Historical Society. They have been exhibited in many places, including the Museum of American Folk Art in New York City and the Museum of Florida History.

Earl Cunningham
*Night Scene*
not dated
Oil on Masonite; 12″ x 22″
Collection of Rubens Teles
Photo by Bill Buckner

Earl Cunningham
*View of the Canal*
not dated
Oil on Masonite; 20″ x 48″
Jay Johnson America's Folk Heritage Gallery
Photo by Bill Buckner

# Ray Cusie

The work of many folk artists is haunted by memories of childhood, of past times and lost friends. The constructions of Ray Cusie are haunted by buildings he has seen. Cusie painstakingly reconstructs these buildings from scraps that he collects while roaming the streets of New York City.

Born in New York City in 1937, Cusie was attracted to its architecture at an early age. By the time he was nine, he was constructing dioramas based on the crumbling buildings that flashed past his eyes as he rode the elevated trains down from his home in the Bronx to Manhattan. As he grew older, he continued to observe city architecture, and over the past decade this interest has flowered into a highly personal art in which he assembles bits of paper, wood, metal, and glass within a picture frame to create from memory a representation of a building or, more often, a group of buildings.

This work combines a love of detail and a fidelity to his material (for a work titled *McCormack's Bar* he employed bits of wood salvaged from the bar itself) with a need, in Cusie's words, "to bring out the feelings and life-styles of city people, past and present." The result is art that is immediately accessible to anyone who has spent much time in a city. The dimly lit doorways, the shrouded halls, the crumbling facades, the faded signs advertising events long past are readily recognizable. These works also have an aura of mystery. A single light glows in an otherwise darkened building. A door stands slightly ajar. Who is there? What is he doing? The fears and doubts of city living flood the works. This mixture of the hidden and the revealed is one of the great strengths of Cusie's works.

Like so many folk artists, Cusie works only part-time. Since 1969, he has been employed in various capacities by the Metropolitan Museum of Art, New York City. He does most of his work at night, bringing to life the buildings he has sketched and photographed during his walks through the city.

Ray Cusie's work is in various collections both here and abroad and has been widely exhibited, particularly in New York City, where it has been seen at, among other places, the Federal Building, the Cork Gallery at Lincoln Center, and the United States Customs House.

Ray Cusie
*Old Americans*
1983
Carved and painted wood;
48″ x 36½″
Collection of Reid and Margaret Morden
Photo by Bill Buckner

# Vestie Davis

Few painters have come to their craft as directly and dramatically as did Vestie Davis. Walking down New York City's 57th Street one day in 1947, he observed a painting in the window of a prestigious gallery, blurted out, "I can paint like that!" and went directly to the nearest art-supplies store. Within a few days he had completed his first work, which he promptly sold—to his insurance agent. After that, he never looked back.

Born in Baltimore, Maryland, in 1903, Davis came to New York City in 1928 and worked for twenty years at such varied trades as circus barker, newsstand manager, and undertaker. Completely unschooled in the arts and without any encouragement, he trained himself to paint and developed a unique style. Discovered by a collector while showing his works at the annual Washington Square Art Show in Manhattan's Greenwich Village, Davis soon found himself featured in an exhibition at the Museum of American Folk Art. From that point until his death in 1978, he worked steadily and productively.

Davis has been referred to as a city primitive, and his canvases reflect the life and times of the great city in which he lived. At first he painted only the buildings and included very few people in his work. He soon found, however, that pictures with people were more popular. A practical fellow ("I paint what the people want, and they want what's familiar to 'em"), Davis began to paint scenes swarming with cheerful if somewhat dowdy New Yorkers. He included dozens and dozens of people on a single canvas: a view of Coney Island by Davis that was used on the September, 1968, cover of *The New Yorker* magazine included five hundred individual figures!

There is much more than "body count" to the work of Vestie Davis. His bright pastel colors, sharply delineated structures, and gay, animated compositions convey a sense of peace and joy. No matter how many figures there are, they do not hurry or behave rudely—they amble along, eating ice cream, holding hands, conveying a sense of peace and well-being.

The manner in which Davis achieved this result was far from haphazard. He was a methodical worker. He would first photograph a scene, then sketch it, and finally transfer the sketch to canvas, carefully indicating on each figure and background element the color it would be painted to assure that clashing ones would not end up side by side. Davis worked for the future. He once declared, "I use very, very good paint—only the best—guaranteed to last."

The paintings of Vestie Davis are widely collected and have been reproduced in such publications as *Newsweek,* the *New York Times,* and *New York* magazine.

Vestie Davis
*Street Scene*
1962
Oil on canvas; 16″ x 24″
Private collection

Vestie Davis
*Luna Park*
1973
Oil on canvas; 17½" x 24"
Collection of Mr. and Mrs.
Kenneth Miller

# William Dawson

William Dawson is one of the few 20th-century folk artists working both as painter and sculptor. Born in Huntsville, Alabama, in 1901, he has lived for many years in Chicago, Illinois. He first attracted attention as a carver but recently has begun to paint, too.

Like so many other folk artists, Dawson turned to art after retirement. He worked for a Chicago produce-distribution plant for many years, and had risen to the position of manager when he retired in the 1960s. Finding that part-time jobs did not satisfy him, he began to attend adult education classes, and these whetted his interest in carving.

Dawson's sculpture focuses on various human and animal forms, houses, and totem poles. The totem poles are his largest works, sometimes exceeding three feet in height. His other pieces are usually quite small, ranging from a few inches to a foot or two in height. Inspiration varies. Some animal forms clearly reflect the sculptor's early life on an Alabama farm. Other pieces, such as the hilarious *Idi Amin Walking His Pet Pig,* reflect Dawson's awareness of current events, particularly television programs. Still other pieces are based on folktales, biblical references, or popular stories.

All of Dawson's works have a powerful totemic quality that is not unlike that of African art. Figures are foreshortened and frontally oriented with a symmetrical organization that is especially noticeable in the totem poles. These often consist of a group of similar heads mounted one atop the next, all of them carved from a single piece of wood (such as a chair leg). Wide, staring eyes and gaping mouths with many shiny white teeth are typical. The eyes mimic, perhaps unconsciously, the cowrie shells used as eyes in African carvings. Dawson's carvings are painted, varnished, and sometimes embellished with bits of shell, stone, feathers, or bone —embellishments that, again, are reminiscent of African examples. The tension in such design is relieved by the constant sense of humor evident in the pieces, as though their creator were saying, "Don't take them all that seriously. I do it for fun."

Dawson's work has been widely exhibited, especially in the Chicago area. Shows in which his works have appeared include *Outsider Art in Chicago,* at the Chicago Museum of Contemporary Art; *Contemporary American Folk and Naive Art,* at the School of the Arts Institute of Chicago. Gallery exhibits of his work have been given at the Phyllis Kind Gallery and the Hyde Park Art Center, both in Chicago.

William Dawson
*Totem Pole*
1982
Carved and painted wood; 41″ high
Private collection

William Dawson
*Untitled*
not dated
Oil on paper; 12″ x 18″
Collection of Dr. Siri von
Reis

# Oscar De Mejo

A folk artist with a truly international reputation, Oscar De Mejo was born in Trieste, Italy, in 1911 and came to the United States in 1947, becoming a citizen five years later. His career over the past thirty years has been one of triumphs seldom accorded folk artists, punctuated by exhibitions at prestigious galleries and major museums both here and abroad.

De Mejo's work, typically done in oils or acrylics on canvas, combines an abiding interest in historical events, especially events related to American history, with a surreal manner of presentation that often leaves the viewer uncertain of the artist's exact meaning. Thus, in *Children of the American Revolution*, Liberty, in the guise of a waitress, enters a room in which a large colonial figure at a piano accompanies a woman singer whose garb and mien are more appropriate to the French Revolution while a child crawls across the floor to seize a sword. The picture is open to various interpretations, but its impact is unquestionable.

In *The Battle of Trenton*, an almost historically accurate portrayal of street fighting is enlivened by the unexpected appearance on the side of the colonials of a towering figure of Liberty bearing a sword and a shield marked with the head of Medusa. Nothing in De Mejo's work can ever be taken for granted.

The impact of his artistry depends not only on subject matter but also on composition and the use of broad planes of bright color. The figures usually appear against a patterned ground: drifted snow, tapestrylike trees or grass, or a checkerboard-painted floor covering. Figures often have exaggerated arms or legs, and the objects around them are disproportionately small. The effect is one of intended disorientation.

Oscar De Mejo's paintings have appeared in many major museums, including the Whitney Museum of American Art in New York City; the Munich Museum; the Palace of Legion of Honor in San Francisco; and the Museum of Lugano, Switzerland, where they were part of the Biennale of Art Naïf in 1972. Among the galleries that have exhibited his work are Carlebach in New York City; the Romi in Paris; and the Stendhal in Milan. He has done work for Hollywood movies, publishing firms, and even magazines, such as *Sports Illustrated*, for which he produced a series of paintings of the Kentucky Derby.

Oscar De Mejo
*Victorian Banquet*
1983
Acrylic on canvas; 36″ x 50″
Aberbach Fine Art

Oscar De Mejo
*Children of the American
Revolution*
1982
Acrylic on canvas; 36" x 50"
Collection of the artist

# John William ("Uncle Jack") Dey

The almost childlike pictures of John William Dey (better known as "Uncle Jack") have an immediate appeal for most collectors of American folk art. Born in 1915, Uncle Jack had an eventful life working at various times as a barber, a policeman, and as a lumberjack in the Maine woods. The time he spent as a lumberjack is particularly evident in his works, which often feature woodland birds and animals —such as crows, woodpeckers, rabbits, and ducks—in a rural or forest setting.

Uncle Jack worked in the unusual medium of airplane enamel, which produces a brittle, glasslike surface reminiscent of cloisonné in its jewellike facets and strongly patterned surface. His paintings were done in great detail and were subjected to a remarkable artistic scrutiny. As the painter noted:

> When I've finished with a painting, I put a bright light on it, and I go over the whole thing with a magnifying glass to see if anything's wrong. Sometimes a picture just doesn't look like it's level, and then I have to put something on to anchor it—something like a cow or a rabbit.

Uncle Jack turned to painting to fill the time after he retired from the police force in 1955. The increasing interest in his art had little effect on him. He painted as he saw fit, when he wanted to, and only what interested him. His wife decided which paintings to keep and which to sell.

An unusual aspect of Uncle Jack's art is that he often painted a picture to fit a particular frame. He would spend days scouring junk shops and secondhand stores to obtain a frame that suited him and then, often in less time than it had taken to find the frame, he would create a work of art perfectly suited to the frame. The size and proportions of the frame and its color and surface texture became integral parts of the painting.

Paintings by Uncle Jack Dey can be found in the collection of the Museum of American Folk Art in New York City and the Museum of International Folk Art in Santa Fe, New Mexico.

John William
("Uncle Jack") Dey
*Portrait of Miles B. Carpenter*
1973
Model airplane paint on board; 20″ x 24″
Collection of Dr. Robert Bishop

# Gisela Fabian

As she once remarked, Gisela Fabian had to open her own art gallery in order to discover that she, too, was an artist. Born in Germany in 1943, she came to the United States at the age of eighteen and by 1972 had established her own gallery on New York's prestigious Madison Avenue.

The gallery was an outgrowth of her interest in collecting primitive Haitian art. Dealing daily with works of art stirred her own artistic impulses and, at the urging of a friend, she finally began to paint. For several years, this work could be carried out only on a part-time basis; in 1980, she gave up the business world and began to devote herself full-time to her painting.

The work of Gisela Fabian is characterized by great detail and sparkling colors that are used to convey messages from what is essentially a dream world. Even where the scene is nominally of Nantucket or upstate New York or some other specific locale, the artist presents it as a fantasy—a childlike vision of nature filled with light and innocence. Other paintings are pure fantasy. Kings, queens, castles, mysterious beasts, and bizarre flowers combine to create a lyrical tapestry of humor and visual poetry.

The humor is often quite subtle. For example, in *Winter Interior*, a painting of a reclining nude (the artist?) is mimicked by a tiny mirrorlike rendition of her lower body set in an alcove high on a wall at the back of the painting.

Paintings by Gisela Fabian have been shown widely, both here and abroad. Among the galleries in which her work has been exhibited are Dietrich-Stone, St. Louis, Missouri; Galerie Pro Arte, Morges, Switzerland; World Gallery, New York City; Anne Cutler, Palm Beach, Florida; Chevron Gallery, San Francisco, California; and Occidental Center Gallery, Los Angeles, California.

Gisela Fabian
*Winter Interior*
1982
Acrylic on canvas; 16" x 20"
Collection of the artist

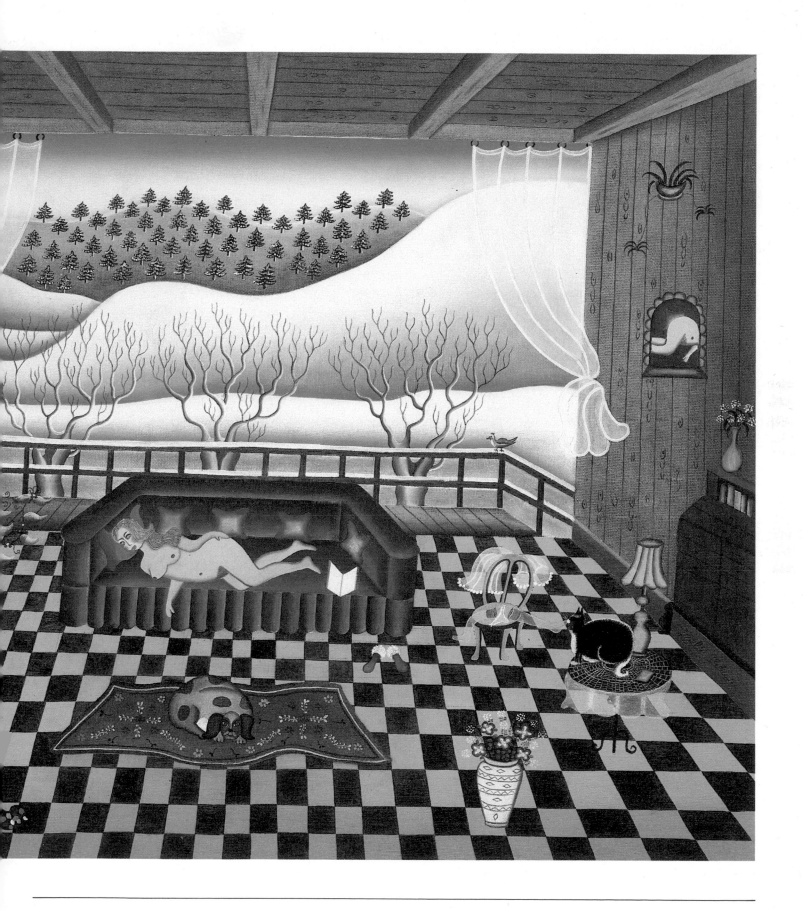

# Barbara Falk

Born in Los Angeles, California, Barbara Falk lived for many years in Connecticut and is now a resident of Tucson, Arizona. She did not begin to paint until she was over forty, by which time she had gone to school, married, and raised a family. Far more articulate than most folk artists in terms of her artistic perceptions and development, Falk attributes this delayed development to her lack of confidence and her unawareness of her own visual perceptions. She notes that, "You have to discover your own identity as a person before anyone is going to discover you as an artist."

Falk did not begin to paint until an art teacher literally forced paint and canvas on her. The teacher offered her neither advice nor instructions. Faced with the challenge, Falk began to paint. At first she painted intimate interiors, such as *By the Window,* peopled by the family and animals she knew and lived with. Although they are perhaps "homey," these paintings are never simply "cute," and their highly stylized composition and dramatic color contrasts immediately draw the viewer's eye.

During the more than ten years that she has been painting, Falk's subject matter and, to some extent, her style have changed. Her strong personal commitment to environmental issues has led her into new fields in which the nature of the material has injected a new and sometimes somber element into her work. In a series called The Elements, she embarked on an exploration of the effect on mankind of uncontrollable natural calamities—earthquakes, tornadoes, and forest fires. In *Tidal Wave,* one of the most dramatic works in this series, she pictures an immense wave of water poised over a neat row of opulent beach houses, among which is a representation of the beach house owned by former President Nixon. The threat is both real and symbolic.

Falk works in acrylics on canvas and usually spends about seven hours a day at her craft, progressing from an idea—often engendered by something seen in the newspaper or heard on a radio talk show—to a completed painting. The entire process may take up to two months and follows a definite progression from an initial sketch of the backgrounds to larger details, such as houses, to the tiny details that constitute the heart of her work. Falk is not a prolific painter.

Paintings by Barbara Falk have been exhibited at the New Britain Museum of American Art, New Britain, Connecticut; the Museum of American Folk Art in New York City; and the John Judkyn Memorial at Freshford Manor, Bath, England. In 1975, she was a recipient of a national art citation from the American Academy and Institute of Arts and Letters. Barbara Falk is also known as Barbara Bustetter Falk.

Barbara Falk
*Tornado*
1975
Acrylic on canvas; 24" x 36"
Collection of Mr. and Mrs. John R. Delfino

Barbara Falk
*Arizona Mining Town*
1979
Acrylic on canvas; 36″ x 48″
Collection of Mr. and Mrs.
Robert Marcus

Barbara Falk
*Burning of Norwalk*
1978
Acrylic on canvas; 44″ x 60″
Collection of Rhonda and
Michael Koulermos

Ralph Fasanella
*Morey Machine Shop*
1955
Oil on canvas; 60″ x 48″
Private collection

# William Fellini

Few fit the stereotypical role of the folk artist as an isolated and misunderstood outsider as well as does William Fellini. Although he appears to have lived most of his adult life in New York City, his date of birth is unknown, his date of death can only be approximated, and the details of his life are sketchy at best. For at least twenty-five years, Fellini worked in New York as a house painter and sometime interior decorator. During much of this period, he painted. His works, which are relatively few in number, include still lifes and landscapes with a strong sense of place and detail that is almost reminiscent of traditional 19th-century painting. Paintings such as *Cabin in the Adirondacks* convey not only the isolation of the "great woods" but also the loneliness of the artist himself, for Fellini's work brought him neither fame nor riches. A long-time acquaintance said of him:

> Our family had known Mr. Fellini for more than twenty-five years, as he worked for my mother as a decorator and "jack of all trades." Without a doubt he was one of the nicest and kindest, a man who was totally misunderstood and not appreciated by his family (artistically). He could not sell one of his pictures during his lifetime. He was so poor he could not afford to buy any new canvas and would often buy used canvas for twenty-five cents and paint on the reverse side. All I can tell you about him is that he was the "Charlie Chaplin" of his group of Third Avenue paint contractors and decorators. They were always teasing him about his "art" work. He never seemed to mind and would say, "Wait, someday these big shots will be surprised!" Well, it's all come true and I'm so sorry he isn't here to enjoy it.

Fellini appears to have worked primarily in oils on canvas, and his style conveys a strong decorative feeling, particularly in the backgrounds, which are often sculptured or "marbleized," quite possibly a reflection of his background as an interior decorator. His paintings have been exhibited at the Museum of American Folk Art in New York City.

*Following page:*
William Fellini
*Still Life, Vase of Flowers*
1936
Oil on Masonite; 11″ x 15″
Museum of American Folk
Art

William Fellini
*Girl Picking Grapes;* 1936
Oil on canvas; 21½″ x 18½″; Museum of American Folk Art

# The Reverend Howard Finster

The religious enthusiasms of the Reverend Howard Finster led him originally into the ministry, where he remained active for some forty years. Age and declining health brought this to an end, however, and he turned to the construction of a garden dedicated to his religious beliefs. In the small Georgia town of Summerville, he began to erect a "Paradise Garden" composed of objects he found in dumps or which were given to him. These he shaped into a fantastic world of towers, walks, and small buildings. Biblical quotations in marbles or fragments of shattered mirrors decorate the paths. Salvaged refrigerator doors were adorned with scripture, concrete walls were reinforced with hubcaps, and photographs of both celebrities and just plain folks were covered with plastic and worked into the composition. A pump house was made of Coca-Cola bottles—all to the glory of the Lord.

Except for a book of drawings done in the 1930s, Finster had not turned his talents to painting. However, in 1976, he began to create religious paintings on various materials. He mounted them under glass salvaged from television screens. Like so much of Finster's activity, this work was inspired: "Back in the winter I got shut in by cold weather, and so these pictures came on my mind, and I began to paint 'em while the cold weather was on, and I just painted a sluice of them."

Finster has worked in a remarkable variety of materials, including oils, house paints, watercolors, and even car lacquer (which he used to protect his first paintings from the weather). He has employed canvas, Masonite, fiberglass, wood, porcelain, and metal. As befits his calling, the Reverend Finster's art is religiously oriented. Some paintings represent illustrations of biblical scripture. Others, such as *There Were Just Enough*, are in the nature of preachments, advice to his flock about how they should live their lives.

Much more than with most folk artists, Finster's art is a part of his life. He paints when inspired, and his wild, baroque creations are a monument to his faith.

Finster's paintings have been widely exhibited, appearing at, among other places, the High Museum of Art in Atlanta; the Library of Congress; the Philadelphia College of Art; and the Abby Aldrich Rockefeller Folk Art Center, Williamsburg, Virginia.

Rev. Howard Finster
*There Were Just Enough*
1970
Enamel on Plexiglas; 20″ x 26″
Private collection
Photo by Bill Buckner

# J. O. J. Frost

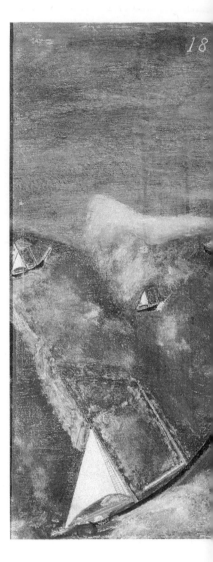

One of the leading folk painters of nautical subjects—a genre relatively uncommon among 20th-century artists in this field—J. O. J. Frost was born in the whaling and shipping town of Marblehead, Massachusetts, in 1852, and died there seventy-six years later. Most of his life was quite ordinary and showed little of the artistic inspiration that was to come. He went to sea at the age of sixteen to help support his widowed mother, but within two years he had decided that there was little profit for the average sailor in cod and halibut fishing.

Fortunately, the father of Frost's sweetheart was a successful restaurateur, and in 1870 Frost left the sea for the dining room, noting later, "It was not through fear of danger, but ambition spurred me on, to get into a better-paid business so I could marry my sweetheart and establish a home." It proved a wise choice. Frost eventually opened his own highly profitable restaurant, remaining active until his retirement, after which he assisted his wife in her florist business.

It was not until 1923, four years after his wife's death, that Frost became interested in art. In August of 1923, a visitor, knowing Frost's previous association with the sea, asked him to sketch a fishing boat of the sort used off the famous Grand Banks. Inspired with the results and recalling what he had seen and experienced in some seventy years in and about Marblehead, Frost embarked on his life's work—some eighty oil paintings in which he recreated the history of the town and her people, from the first settlers in 1625 to the conflicts with the Indians, the Revolution, and the constant struggle for survival against the sea and a hostile climate. The ongoing panorama ended only when the artist died in 1928.

Frost's paintings are filled with activity—fishing vessels battling rough seas, troops mustering on the village common—and a feeling of vibrant life that is accented both by the artist's frenetic line and by his choice of bright colors. Where the subject dealt with cannot be completely encompassed visually, notes written on the canvas as part of the composition continue the tale. It is like a history book come to life.

In 1926, Frost opened his own gallery, the "new art building," in which to display his work. Since then, paintings by Frost have been exhibited at various museums, including the Whitney Museum of American Art in New York City, and can be found in both public and private collections.

J. O. J. Frost
*Ships in a Gale*
1925
Oil on canvas; 32½″ x 64½″
Private collection

# Carlton Elonzo Garrett

Born and raised in Georgia, Carlton Elonzo Garrett did not begin to carve until 1980, when he was eighty years old, but in the few years that he has been active, his work has attracted national interest. Garrett produces small, doll-like figures the faces of which are imbued with remarkable character. Though he does individuals, he is clearly most at home with groups. Complex scenes mounted on platforms, such as *The Hospital* or *Mount Opel, The Holy Children of Israel,* sometimes contain over two dozen individual figures, each with its own personality and each interacting with other actors in the drama.

The subject matter of these dioramas reflects the artist's background. Brought up in rural Georgia and unable to either read or write, Garrett draws most of his inspiration from his home and church life. His experience as a worker in flour and furniture mills provided him with some technical background and a familiarity with tools. It also gave him another source of inspiration: machinery. Works like *The Watermill* and *Machinery* are almost in the nature of toys and may reflect the sculptor's familiarity as a child with the tin steam-engine toys so popular during the 1920s and 1930s.

As a part-time preacher for a fundamentalist Christian sect, Garrett has also been greatly interested in things of the spirit, and works like *The Crucifixion* combine a moving sense of faith with a charmingly naive composition.

Garrett works in wood, which he paints and sometimes combines with other materials, such as tin and wire. His workshop is a shed behind his home, and he works when it suits him. Even at his advanced age, family and church life are still the center of his existence.

Carvings by Carlton Elonzo Garrett can be found in the permanent collections of the High Museum of Art in Atlanta and the Museum of International Folk Art, Santa Fe, New Mexico. He has been interviewed on the "Today Show," and his works have appeared in *Popular Mechanics* magazine.

*Left:* Carlton Elonzo Garrett
*Mount Opel, The Holy Children of Israel*
not dated
Carved and painted wood;
46″ x 31½″ x 34¼″
Collection of Judith Alexander
Photo by Ed Thompson
*Above:* Carlton Elonzo Garrett
Detail of *Mount Opel, The Holy Children of Israel*

# Victor Joseph Gatto

One of the greatest folk painters of this century, Victor Joseph Gatto was born in New York City in 1893 and lived there most of his life, retiring to Miami, Florida, only a short time before his death in 1965.

Unlike the many folk painters and sculptors who turned to art upon retirement from their primary careers, Gatto was always obsessed with it. When he was a child, one of his drawings was seen in a school exhibition by President Theodore Roosevelt. Roosevelt prophesied a great career as an artist for Gatto, a prediction that was a long time in fulfillment: Gatto was forty-five before he began to paint seriously. Before this he had lost his mother, spent some time in an orphanage, boxed professionally, served in the U.S. Navy, and worked at various jobs, including plumber and steamfitter. None of this either satisfied him or brought him profit. In 1938, when he began to paint full-time, he was a poor man.

Chancing upon an art show in New York's Greenwich Village, Gatto asked an exhibitor if anyone ever bought the paintings. Upon learning they did, he promptly bought the necessary materials and began to paint. Within a fairly short period of time, Gatto had begun to attract critical attention, and in the early 1940s a picture of his appeared in the prestigious Whitney Museum of American Art. He had a one-man show at the Charles Barzansky Gallery in 1943 and was thereafter a major figure.

Gatto's paintings, particularly his oils, are remarkably complex. Using brushes with only a few hairs in order to achieve great detail, and building up layer after layer of paint in an impasto effect, he created works of monumental detail. One, *Circus at the Garden,* included the figures of no fewer than 18,000 spectators; another, *Knights Jousting,* took four years to complete. Gatto's paintings fell into two broad categories: genre scenes, such as *Circus, Rockefeller Plaza,* and *Washington Square,* in which he captured the vibrancy and life of New York City; and fantasies, which were often based on biblical subjects.

Although he worked slowly, Gatto was tireless—often toiling at the easel for thirty-six hours straight—and unsparing of himself. When his eyesight began to fail, he continued to paint, employing a magnifying glass. And he was rewarded for his dedication. During his lifetime his works were purchased by many wealthy collectors, and today they hang in such prestigious institutions as the Whitney Museum of American Art and the Museum of the City of New York.

Victor Joseph Gatto; *Nightmare;* not dated
Oil on canvas board; 16″ x 20″; Epstein/Powell American Primitives
Photo by D. James Dee

Victor Joseph Gatto
*Untitled*
1962
Pen on paper; 8½″ x 11″
Epstein/Powell American
Primitives
Photo by D. James Dee

# Esther Gyory

The works of Esther Gyory combine the rich folk traditions of her native country with the spirit and inspiration of her adopted land. Born in Budapest, Hungary, in 1944, of a Hungarian father and an American mother, Gyory came to this country in 1966. Although her uncle Ferenc Medgyesy was a well-known sculptor and a source of inspiration to her, she did not begin to paint until 1975, when the death of her mother caused her to reevaluate her goals. She turned to art, drawing on the rich folk tradition of Hungary.

It would not be accurate, however, to characterize Gyory's work as pure memory painting. Although she draws heavily on her European background, she is largely unconcerned with details of dress or locale, and scenes, figures, and incidents that occur in her dreams serve as crucial elements in many of her paintings. Gyory is deeply involved in spiritual and mystical life, and this is reflected in her paintings to the extent that a figure or occurrence may represent for her much more than it may appear to if one interprets the canvas literally.

These deep feelings are reflected not only in the contents of a picture but in its size, too. The artist notes, "When I'm in a good mood and confident, I paint large size. If something is depressing me, I tend to go to smaller sizes."

Gyory lives and works in her studio in New York City, employing an unusual combination of oils and acrylics on canvas. The bright colors and great activity found in her paintings may reflect the joy of a village dance or the preparation of the year's wine, but they may also mask the horror and cruelty of a pig being butchered. Unlike some folk artists, Gyory understands only too well that country life is not all pleasantness.

Gyory's paintings are in various public and private collections, including that of the John Judkyn Memorial at Freshford Manor, Bath, England. Her works have been exhibited at the Columbus Museum of Art, Columbus, Ohio; the Salmagundi Club, New York City; the Kar Gallery of Fine Art, Toronto, Canada; and the Frontier Hotel Art Gallery, Las Vegas, Nevada.

Esther Gyory
*Vineyard*
1978
Acrylic and oil on canvas; 28" x 30"
Private collection

Esther Gyory
*Amish Farm*
1980
Acrylic and oil on canvas; 16" x 20"
Collection of Mr. and Mrs. Jim Frink

Esther Gyory
*The Pig Killing*
1979
Acrylic and oil on canvas;
20″ x 24″
Private collection

# Morris Hirshfield

In a very real sense, the life of Morris Hirshfield is the immigrant's dream come true. Born in 1872 in a small Polish town near what was then the German border, he came to the United States at the age of eighteen. He settled in New York City and found work in a factory making women's coats. Some years later, he became co-owner, with his brother, of a similar business. He later entered the slipper-manufacturing business and became the largest maker of slippers in New York. In 1937, he was forced to retire because of poor health, and he turned to art.

His initial efforts were a disappointment to him. He once wrote to the gallery owner Sidney Janis, "It seems that my mind knew well what I wanted to portray, but my hands were unable to produce what my mind demanded." However, by 1939, Hirshfield had reached the point where two of his paintings were selected for the exhibition *Unknown Americans*, held at New York's Museum of Modern Art. During the remaining seven years of his life, he completed over seventy paintings, was given a retrospective at the Museum of Modern Art in 1943, and emerged as one of the major folk artists of this century.

The work of Morris Hirshfield, primarily executed in oils on canvas, is a charming mixture of the bizarre and the decorative. Animals and female nudes particularly interested him, and they are often combined, as in *The Artist and His Model*, in which Hirshfield portrays himself in the act of painting a voluptuous model while an equally voluptuous cat stares down from a picture on the wall that serves as background to the scene. The artist's colors are strong and boldly placed, and background elements are often highly patterned, as in *Girl with Her Dog*, in which the large figures stand out against a wall of tiny stars and dots. Sidney Janis traced this sense of ground and texture to Hirshfield's background in the textile business: his textured surfaces came from fabrics; his design from pattern making.

Paintings by Morris Hirshfield have been exhibited at various institutions, including the Whitney Museum of American Art, the Museum of Modern Art, and the Philadelphia College of Art.

Morris Hirshfield
*Landscape*
1941
Oil on canvas; 26¼″ x 34″
Collection of Richard and Suzanne Barancik
Photo by David R. Williams

Morris Hirshfield
*Girl with Her Dog*
1943
Oil on canvas; 45½″ x 35½″
The Bragaline Collection

# Clementine Hunter

Often referred to as "the black Grandma Moses," Clementine Hunter was born about 1885 at Hidden Hill Plantation near Natchitoches, Louisiana. At the age of sixteen, she moved to the nearby Melrose Plantation, where she worked for many years as a field hand. In her early sixties, she became a kitchen and laundry worker at Melrose, one of the owners of which was an amateur painter and patron of the arts. Although it is doubtful that the presence of academic artists influenced Hunter's work, it did offer her both the opportunity to find materials and the idea that she, too, might paint. One day, she picked up a few partially used tubes of oil paints and, with a window shade as canvas, she created her first work—a plantation baptism scene.

Since that first work, this illiterate but creative woman has produced over 4,000 paintings of various sizes on various materials, including cardboard, plywood, and brown paper bags. She sold many of her first works for a dime or a quarter to pay for medical treatment for her ailing husband or to buy clothes for her grandchildren. Many of these early works have been rescued from the obscurity of sharecroppers' cabins. By the 1950s, Hunter was making a name for herself outside the narrow confines of the Louisiana backwater. In 1956, the New Orleans Museum of Art honored her with a one-woman show, the first show for a black artist ever given at that institution. In 1976, her *Threshing Pecans* was chosen to be used on UNICEF Christmas cards. By that time, collectors throughout the South were seeking her simple but moving paintings.

Hunter earns a modest living and lives in a trailer with running water and electricity, amenities never available to her in the wooden shack in which she did her first paintings. That shack is now being preserved by a local historical society.

Hunter's paintings are characterized by a childlike simplicity and directness and a sensitive use of color. She paints what she knows and has experienced: childhood life among black plantation workers, with scenes of weddings, baptisms, religious revival meetings, field work, dances, and even funerals. All of her works are imbued with a feeling of hope and joy that one is surprised to find among those so economically deprived.

The paintings of Clementine Hunter have been exhibited at the Museum of American Folk Art in New York City and at the New Orleans Museum of Art and are in the collections of various collectors and institutions.

Clementine Hunter
*Funeral*; 1956
House paint on cardboard; 18″ x 24″
Collection of Dr. Siri von Reis; photo by Bill Buckner

# Lola K. Isroff

Rather than being driven to it by some inner compulsion, Lola Isroff came to art quite by accident. Born in New York City in 1920 and well educated, she planned to pursue a career as a writer and, indeed, spent six years on the editorial staff of *The New Yorker* magazine. In the course of doing research for a planned historical novel, she began to visit early 19th-century houses in Manhattan. One of these so impressed her that she found she could not express her feelings in words. She decided to sketch the building. Returning home, she touched up the sketch with watercolors and was astounded at the result.

Since writing was hard for her, and she found painting easy, Isroff became a painter. She began painting old houses and interiors, first in Manhattan and then, after a move with her husband to Ohio, in the rural Midwest. Her career was given a major boost in 1950, when she won one of the prizes in the *Art News* National Amateur Painter Competition and the painting she had submitted was used by the U.S. State Department to illustrate an article in a Voice of America publication.

Lola K. Isroff
*Red Chair in Meadow*
not dated
Watercolor on paper; 9″ x 11¾″
Private collection

Lola K. Isroff
*Port Scene, Venezuela*
not dated
Oil on canvas board; 14″ x
18″
Collection of the artist

In 1976, her watercolor *Girl at Desk* was chosen to illustrate the UNICEF calendar.

Isroff now lives in Akron, Ohio, where she has a studio in her apartment and works in acrylics on canvas or paper and in watercolors. She confines her work almost exclusively to old houses and interiors and finds that she can paint only those scenes that, as she expresses it, "draw me." "Call it what you will," she remarks, "but a house has to have a special something to make me want to sketch it. Without that rapport, my pencil refuses to budge."

Fortunately, Isroff has been inspired often enough for her to have created a sizable body of work, examples from which are included in the collection of the Musée d'Art Naïf de l'Ile de France, Paris. Among her more than a dozen one-woman exhibitions have been those at the Akron Art Museum, Lord & Taylor in New York City, and the Vault Galleries in Boston.

# Kathy Jakobsen

One of the youngest of the contemporary folk painters and one of the most widely collected, Kathy Jakobsen was born in Wyandotte, Michigan, in 1952. She now lives and works in the Chelsea area of New York City.

The extraordinary visual appeal of her works has caused some authorities to liken them to ancient manuscript illuminations; others see in her paintings a continuation of the Pennsylvania Fraktur tradition. Her own views are much simpler. While admitting to an interest in calligraphy, which is reflected in the remarkable detail of her work, she views her paintings as a message from her to the onlooker. "I think paintings are food for the spirit. They should communicate to the viewer, and the viewer should be able to contribute and share in or relate to the painting. It is a two-way thing."

Brought up in Michigan, she spent a great deal of time both in the woods and in observing the Victorian architecture so common in that area. Her work reflects both influences. Paintings such as *Ice Fishing in Michigan* memorialize traditional rural sporting activities, and the incredibly ornate buildings in many of her compositions reflect her early interest in the Victorian style.

Jakobsen is not a memory painter in the traditional sense. While her work does reflect her grandparents' tales of early Michigan, she is constantly seeking new inspiration. Paintings such as *South Street Seaport* and *The Plaza* indicate her developing interest in the architecture of Manhattan, where she now lives.

The appeal of her work lies not only in the brilliant colors and the great detail but also in the combination of activity and peace. A large composition like *Broadway* or *The Plaza* will be filled with activity—people and animals—but will also always possess a feeling of tranquility quite foreign to most urban scenes. The viewer is not threatened by these paintings.

Kathy Jakobsen works in oils on canvas, and she is one of the most widely collected of the current folk artists. Her paintings are in, among others, the Henry Ford Museum, Dearborn, Michigan; the Smithsonian Institution, Washington, D.C.; the Museum of American Folk Art, New York City; and the John Judkyn Memorial, Freshford Manor, Bath, England. They have been exhibited in dozens of shows throughout the United States and western Europe and are in many collections, including that of Mrs. Betty Ford.

Kathy Jakobsen
*The Plaza*
1981
Oil on canvas; 30" x 40"
Collection of Dr. and Mrs.
Howard Pottak
Photo by Bill Buckner

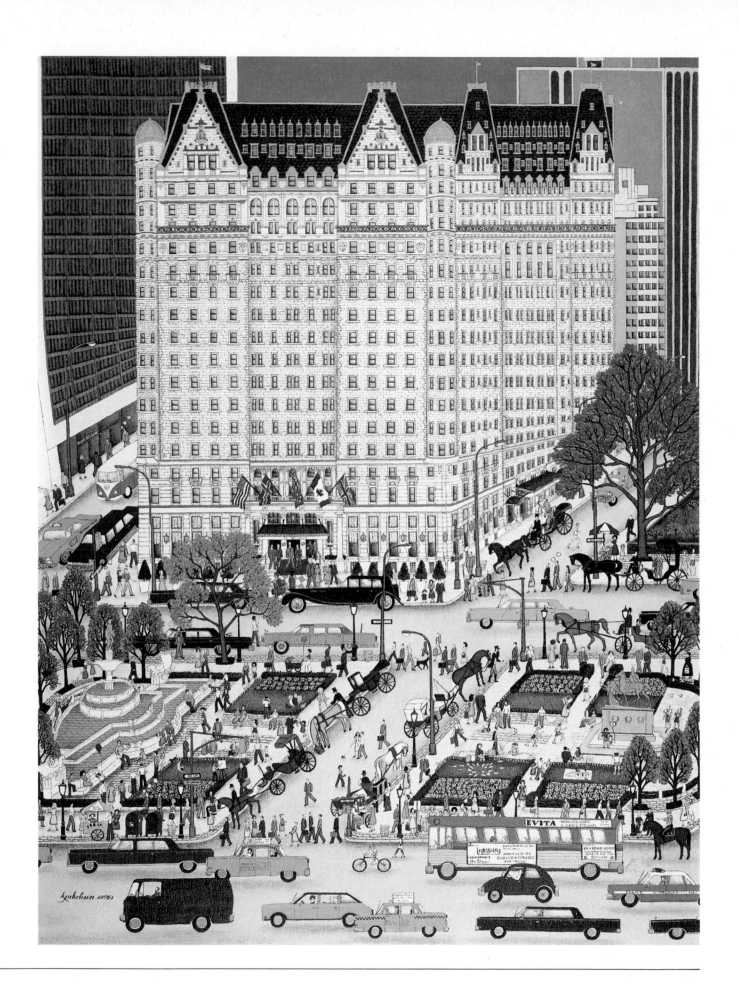

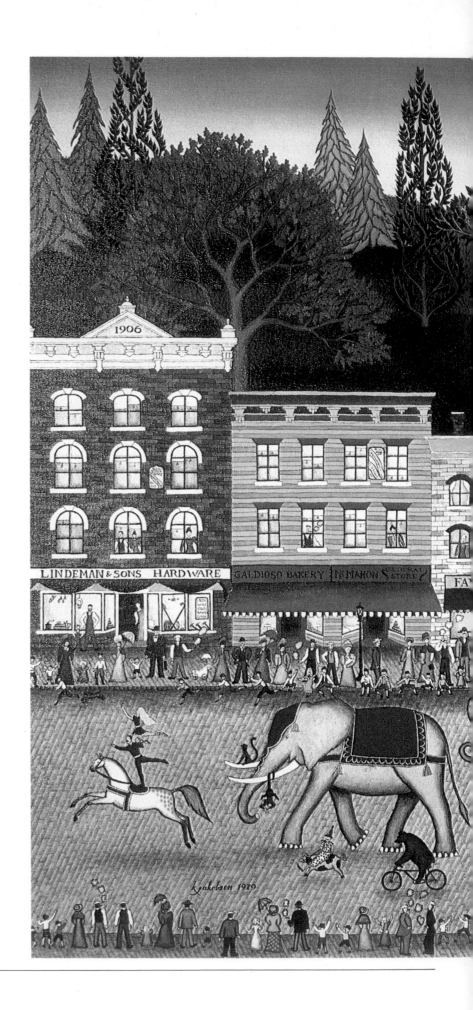

Kathy Jakobsen
*Circus Parade*
1979
Oil on canvas; 30″ x 40″
Collection of Werner and Karen Gundersheimer

Kathy Jakobsen
*Eve in the Garden*
1981
Oil on canvas; 30″ x 40″
Collection of Mr. and Mrs.
David Hartfield, Jr.
Photo by Bill Buckner

# Theodore Jeremenko

Born in Yugoslavia in 1938, Theodore Jeremenko came to the United States in 1950 and now resides in New York City with a second home at East Hampton on nearby Long Island. His first trips to Long Island provided the initial inspiration for his work. Impressed by the beauty of the seacoast and by the way the local buildings seemed to relate to their surroundings, he began to compose landscapes based on this subject matter.

Jeremenko's paintings are highly architectural in nature, which is not surprising in light of his avowed interest in the restoration of old homes and in the field of architecture itself. Indeed, some of his pieces have the quality of an architectural rendering. Severely delineated buildings form geometric designs against a darkened and clearly secondary background. Streets and fields are usually devoid of human or animal figures. The buildings are clearly preeminent.

Jeremenko is meticulous in his approach to a painting. He works from nature, first sketching the scene he wishes to recreate, noting the colors of trees and buildings, then rearranging this material to suit his own artistic impulses. This rearrangement includes the removal of all modern elements, such as gas tanks and telephone lines, in order to restore the scene to a 19th-century mood. The results are stark and moving representations of a New England that might have been, or, perhaps, never was. Jeremenko's works offer us the essence of that coastal area.

Works by Theodore Jeremenko are in various private collections, and they have been exhibited at several galleries, including Gallery East in East Hampton, New York; Gallery North at Setauket, New York; and Marie Pellicone, New York City.

Theodore Jeremenko
*Near the Ocean*
1982
Acrylic on canvas; 11″ x 16″
Collection of Mr. and Mrs.
David Ginzberg
Photo by Bill Buckner

Theodore Jeremenko
*Six Trees*
1983
Acrylic on canvas; 21″ x 25″
Private collection
Photo by Bill Buckner

# S. L. Jones

The carver Shields Landon Jones, known as S. L. Jones, was born in Franklin County, Virginia, the son of a sharecropper and one of thirteen children. Before he was a teenager, the family bought a small farm in Summers County, West Virginia. In 1918, at the age of seventeen, Jones left school and the farm to go to work on the railroad. Life in the West Virginia mountains was hard, and railroad work was often dangerous, but life had its compensations: hunting and music. It was while watching for deer and treeing possum that Jones started to pass the time by carving small figures; and there was music everywhere—in the church, in the grange hall, and in the home. By the time he was ten, Jones was an accomplished fiddler and banjo player.

Hunting, forest animals, fiddling contests, and the railroad are common themes in Jones's work, but he is best known for his portrait heads. Using native hardwoods such as maple or walnut or the softer poplar and working now with professional wood chisels rather than the pocketknife of years past, Jones sculpts massive heads that reflect the abstracted faces and personalities of people he has known or visions that have come to him in dreams. He works in a studio he built himself on the rise behind his small house at Pine Hill, West Virginia, on the slopes of the Blue Ridge Mountains.

Jones's work is sometimes compared with that of contemporary academic sculptors such as Elie Nadelman and Alexander Calder, but he is entirely self-trained, and his use of frontal positioning, broad flat surfaces, and foreshortened torsos reflects his own solutions to artistic problems rather than reliance on the advice or experience of others. His themes, such as the fiddler and the hunter with his dog, express a life experience alien to almost all academic artists.

The work of S. L. Jones has been widely exhibited during the past decade (he began to carve seriously in the early 1970s). His sculpture and the drawings he also does can be found in the permanent collections of the Smithsonian Institution, Washington, D.C.; and the Museum of American Folk Art, New York City. His works have been shown throughout the United States and in Europe and Japan.

S. L. Jones
*Untitled*
1980
Carved and painted wood;
12″ x 15″ x 11″
Epstein/Powell American
Primitives

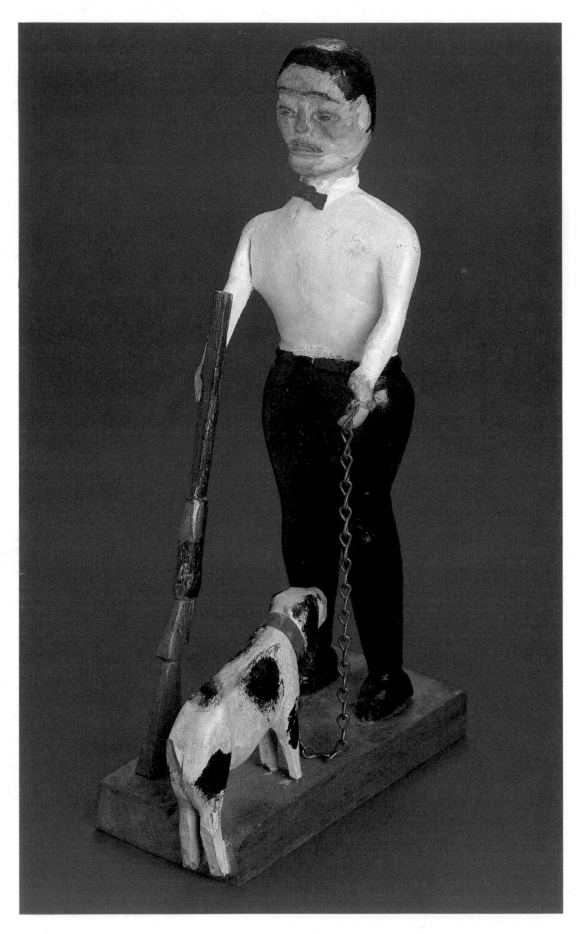

S. L. Jones
*Hunter and Dog*
not dated
Carved and painted wood;
12″ high
Collection of Mr. and Mrs.
Gerhard Stebich
Photo by Bill Buckner

# Andy Kane

Born in New York City in 1956, Andy Kane spent many of his early summers on Long Island and at the various amusement parks, such as Coney Island, scattered along New York's oceanfront. Fascinated by the sights, sounds, and colors of the midway, he developed a style emphasizing strong color and movement with seemingly irreconcilable elements held together by borders of repeated motifs, such as palm trees, tulips, or even human figures. These paintings have the quality of a painting on tapa cloth or a batik print.

Frequently left alone after the early death of his mother, Kane began devoting himself to drawing and painting. He dropped out of school at the age of sixteen and spent months wandering across the United States and Canada, storing up the visual images now being released through his canvases.

His works have a pictographlike quality, blending stick figures, broad areas of strong color, and an iconography suitable to the message to be conveyed. Thus, in *Welcome To N.Y.C.*, a subway train rolls across the center of the picture while above it tower the cluttered buildings of the city and below, evident only to the cognoscenti, a line of cockroaches passes in review.

Kane's work is included in the collection of the Museum of American Folk Art in New York City and has been shown at the Janet Fleisher Gallery, Philadelphia; Webb & Parsons, New Canaan, Connecticut; and in Jay Johnson America's Folk Heritage Gallery, New York City.

Andy Kane
*Welcome To N.Y.C.*
1977
Oil on canvas; 30″ x 40″
Jay Johnson America's Folk
Heritage Gallery

Andy Kane
*Stage in the Sun*
1977
Oil on canvas; 30″ x 36″
Private collection

# John Kane

One of the first folk artists in America to gain national recognition, John Kane was born in Scotland in 1870 and came to this country at the age of nineteen. For many years, he supported himself as a miner, a laborer on the railroads, a street paver, and a steel-mill hand. He boxed as an amateur and wandered back and forth across Alabama, Kentucky, and Tennessee, his restlessness exacerbated by the death, in 1904, of an infant son.

Kane's raw natural talent began to take shape when he got a job painting the exteriors of railway freight cars. In his own words, "The next job I had was the one contributed most of all towards my artistic work. I became a painter. I painted freight cars. The best thing in the world for a young artist would be to hire himself out to a good painting contractor."

Thereafter, he worked at other related crafts, including house painting and the retouching and repainting of photographs. It may have been through this employment that he added to his wonderful sense of color and composition the draftsmanship so evident in *Self-Portrait* and other works and so often lacking in the work of most folk artists. That all these related jobs sharpened his eye and trained his hand is evident from Kane's own evaluation:

> I believe many a young art student would profit greatly if he learned to paint as an outdoor painter does rather than confine his training to the art school. They never teach how to get those colors for themselves. A house painter knows how to get it for himself. Often I have been at a loss to know how to overcome some significant point in artistic form which I would have learned easily in an art school. But my spirit of observation has helped me to acquire knowledge and so the source of my information did not matter.

Kane's career as a painter received a major boost in 1928, when Pittsburgh's Carnegie Institute purchased one of his paintings. Unfortunately, by then he had little time left. He died in Pittsburgh in 1934, leaving behind a body of work, primarily oils on canvas and composition board, that is regarded as among the finest of the genre ever produced in this country.

John Kane
*Self-Portrait*
1929
Oil on canvas over composition board; 36⅛" x 27⅛"
Museum of Modern Art, New York; Abby Aldrich Rockefeller Fund

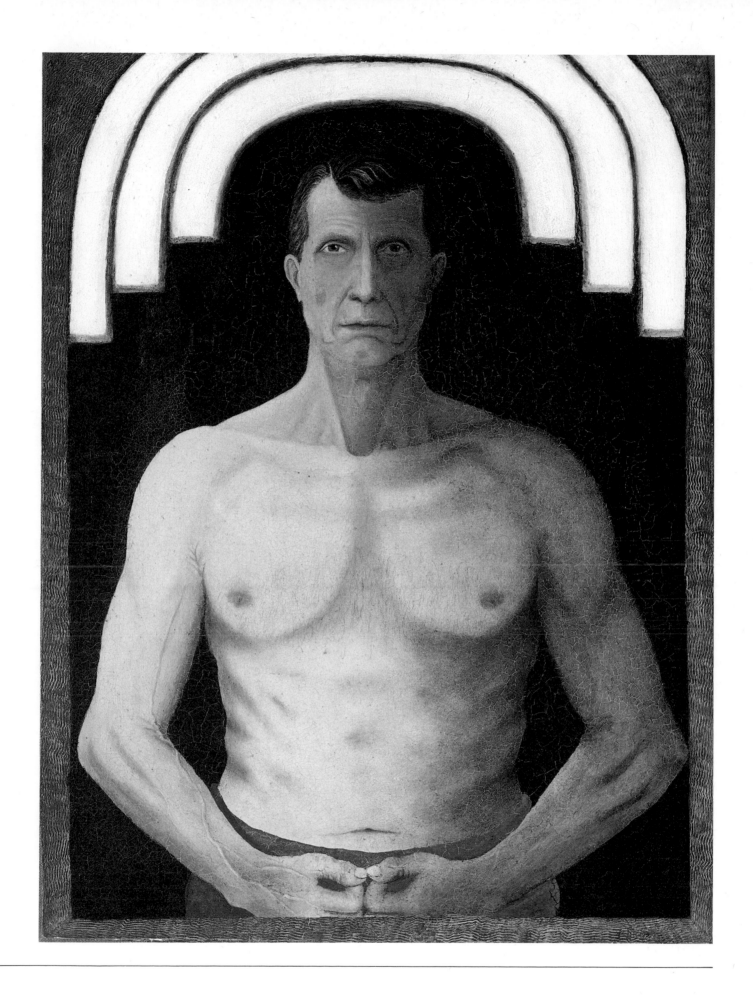

# Marie Keegan

When she was in her early twenties, Marie Keegan was told by a fortune teller that her "fortune was in her hands." Keegan thought the fortune teller was referring to the IBM Keypunch Service Bureau that she was running at the time. In later years, Keegan came to feel that the prophesy had referred to something very different— her gift of artistry, which she did not discover until she was well into her thirties, when she had a home, a husband, and children.

It was the home, in fact, that initially inspired her. When her family moved to Stockholm, New Jersey, she found herself in a house overlooking a lovely lake. Keegan was born in 1941 in New York City, and the rural beauty around her in her new home seemed like such a great contrast to the city that it called for some response from her. That response came in the form of paintings, oils on canvas, which began as pure landscapes but later evolved into busy woodland scenes, such as *Gathering of Maple Syrup,* and even interiors, such as the remarkably symmetrical *Circus.*

Keegan's work is based to some extent on her observation of rural New Jersey, but it is much more the product of reworking rural history, of "how things used to be." Thus, in *Sussex Ice Company,* she recreates the old-time custom of cutting and storing pond ice for summer use. Whatever the theme, however, her work is marked by rich and sensitively used colors, a symmetrically patterned background —which can be composed of trees or even the heads of people in an audience— and great attention to detail.

Keegan's studio is her dining room overlooking the lake she loves so well, and her working hours are those when she is free of family responsibilities. Although she loves her work, she is not obsessed by it. It remains part of her very full life.

Marie Keegan's work is part of the collection of the John Judkyn Memorial, Freshford Manor, Bath, England, and has been exhibited in numerous places in England, including Woodspring Museum, Weston-super-Mare, and the University of East Anglia at Norwich.

Marie Keegan
*Circus Parade*
1980
Oil on canvas; 18″ x 24″
Collection of Rubens Teles
Photo by Bill Buckner

Marie Keegan
*Gathering of Maple Sugar*
1980
Oil on canvas; 24" x 30"
Collection of Gray Boone

Marie Keegan
*A Farm in New Jersey*
1982
Oil on canvas; 30" x 36"
Collection of Noeli Clemente Sergio

# Tella Kitchen

Tella Kitchen came late to her calling as folk painter. Born in 1902 on a farm in the rolling hills of Vinton County, Ohio, she spent her formative years in rural America, first near Londonderry, Ohio, and then at Independence, Indiana. At the age of eighteen, she married Noland Kitchen and returned to Ohio, where they raised four children. After her husband's death in 1963, she succeeded him as mayor of the small community in which they lived and continued an active life surrounded by grandchildren and over a dozen great-grandchildren.

This busy life was not enough for her, and as she looked for ways to spend her time she found herself thinking more and more of the events of her childhood and wishing for a way to show her family how life had been back then. A way was opened when a son presented her with a set of paints, but a single lesson with a professional instructor convinced Kitchen that, in her words, "I was too old to paint newfangled things, and I just began to paint the simple things I remembered and loved."

Combining her rich store of memories with an instinctive feeling for color and composition, Kitchen has brought to life the midwestern America of the early 20th century. In works like *The Burning of Buck's Livery Stable, Independence, Indiana* and *The Knights of Phythias Fair Held in the Strouse Grove,* she recaptures the times of crisis and the moments of fleeting joy that were so much a part of growing up in the farm belt. Her pictures are filled with details—running horses, groups of people, steam locomotives, and the variety of animals common to a rural community. The concern for historical accuracy typical of many memory painters does not stand in the way of Kitchen's powerful sense of design. She remains a painter first, a historian second.

Tella Kitchen is represented in many public and private collections, including the Museum of International Folk Art, Santa Fe, New Mexico; the Antique Monthly Collection of American Folk Art from the South; and the Golden Lamb Inn, at Lebanon, Ohio.

Tella Kitchen
*Rail Road Station on the*
*Wabash River at Riverside,*
*Indiana*
1975
Oil on canvas; 22″ x 28″
© Tella Kitchen
Collection of Mr. and Mrs.
C. V. Hagler

Tella Kitchen
*When the Fred Buck Livery
Stable Burned*
1976
Oil on canvas; 30″ x 40″
© Tella Kitchen
Collection of Werner and
Karen Gundersheimer

# Gustav Klumpp

Gustav Klumpp was one of the most single-minded of the 20th century's folk artists. During his career, he focused almost exclusively on female nudes or on group nude scenes, such as *Dream of a Nudist Camp Wedding.* This predilection would not have brought Klumpp to prominence had it not been coupled with a remarkable sense of color and design that has earned him a permanent place in the annals of folk painting.

Born in Germany in 1902, Klumpp came to the United States in 1923 and worked, until his retirement in 1964, as a compositor and linotype operator, crafts for which he had been trained in his native land. Casting about for something to do after retirement, Klumpp joined a senior citizen center, and, in 1966, its director suggested that Klumpp try painting. Though he had no background in the field and until then had had no specific interest in painting, Klumpp found himself drawn to painting. His first work, a copy of a portrait of Abraham Lincoln, was realistic, but he quickly moved into the world of fantasy and, specifically, to the painting of unclothed young women.

When asked about this "specialty" of his, Klumpp responded:

My philosophy of art painting which is expressed in the visualization of painting beautiful girls in the nude or seminude and in fictitious surroundings including some other paintings of dreamlike nature. This is one reason I love to paint and I was trying to accomplish something particular at the golden age and as an inspiration to other senior citizens or the younger generation. To beautify and enhance the place where it is displayed.

Though he focused on the nude, Klumpp used the human figure as one part of a highly sophisticated compositional framework within which he expressed his wonderful sense of humor, his political beliefs, and his comments on human society. But over all there was the woman, epitomized, perhaps, in his *The Art Gallery Saluting the Nude,* in which a large reclining nude (a painting within a painting) looms over a group of tiny viewers, among whom are a pair of saluting servicemen —a pun, perhaps, on the salty old military joke.

Paintings by Gustav Klumpp can be found in the Museum of International Folk Art, Santa Fe, New Mexico.

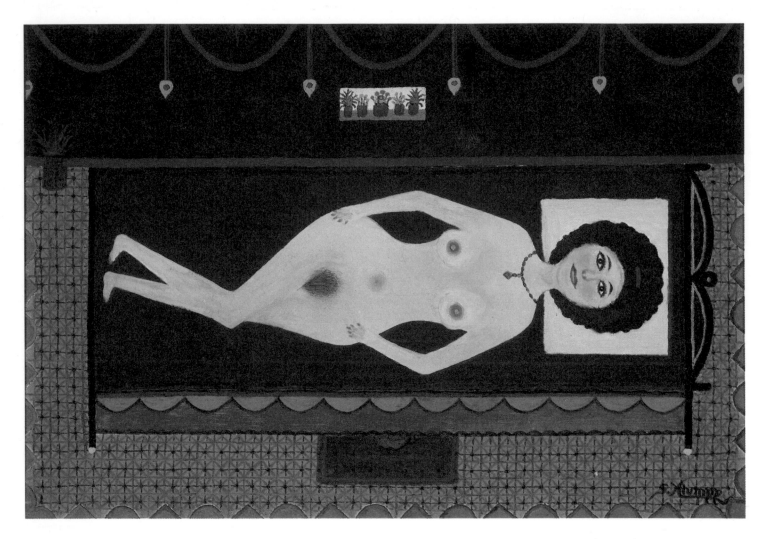

Gustav Klumpp
*Reclining Nude*
1970
Oil on canvas; 14″ x 20″
Jay Johnson America's Folk
Heritage Gallery
Photo by Bill Buckner

Gustav Klumpp
*Beauty Contest*
1971
Oil on canvas; 14″ x 18″
Collection of Dorothy and
Leo Rabkin
Photo by Bill Buckner

# Olof Krans

The Swedish-born artist Olof Krans is generally recognized as having been one of the leading lights of the 20th-century folk movement. Born Olof Olson in Silja, Sweden, in 1838, he came with his family in 1850 to Bishop Hill, a communal society established in central Illinois by Swedish religious dissenters. Though his artistic talents had been recognized at an early age, Krans spent his youth working as a farm hand and blacksmith's helper at Bishop Hill.

By the time of the Civil War, the community, though it had prospered economically, had foundered on religious and political differences. Taking the name Krans, Olof joined the Union Army. After returning from service, he married and worked first as a traveling photographer and later as a painter of houses, signs, and even stage backdrops.

The skills he learned stood Krans in good stead when he turned his hand, in the 1890s, to portrait and genre painting. It appears that he had always painted a bit, but two events—a crippling injury that prevented active work and the approach of the celebration of the fiftieth anniversary of the founding of Bishop Hill—caused him, in 1896, to take up his brush in earnest.

Krans embarked on his most important work, a series of oils on canvas tracing the settlement and growth of the community. Today, paintings such as *Harvesting Grain* and *Women Driving Piling* rank among the most important examples of American folk art. Many of these "documentary" works were done from photographs, but Krans's unique sense of design and organization transcended the materials from which he worked.

During the years 1896 to 1911, Krans produced numerous views of old Bishop Hill, almost all of which he gave to the community's Old Settlers' Association, and some sixty portraits of early inhabitants of the community. The portraits were taken from photographs from the period 1860 to 1870, thus providing an interesting link between Krans's former occupation as photographer and his later one of painter.

Olof Krans lived most of his life in Ohio and Illinois. He died in Altona, Illinois, in 1916. His paintings are in the collections of the Illinois Department of Conservation; Bishop Hill State Historic Site; the Chicago Historical Society; and various individuals. A major retrospective of his work was held at the Museum of American Folk Art in New York City in 1982.

Olof Krans
*Harvesting Grain*
ca. 1900
Oil on canvas; 29½″ x 47″
Bishop Hill Memorial, Illinois Department of Conservation

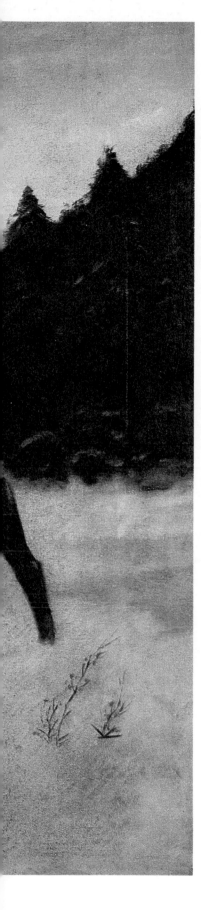

Olof Krans
*Bear and Elk Fighting*
ca. 1905
Oil on canvas; 30″ x 36½″
Collection of Mr. Merle Glick

Olof Krans
*Portrait of Peter Krans*
ca. 1902
Oil on canvas; 18″ x 24″
Collection of Mr. Merle Glick

# Rose Labrie

Rose Labrie is probably the quintessential memory painter. In her own words: "I paint primitives because I paint my memories." Born in Boston, she moved, in 1918, to rural Vermont, where her close-knit family lived in a great grambrel-roofed house overlooking pond, barns, fields, and forest. Her varied works are a reflection of that life.

It was not until some fifteen years ago—after an already full life raising a family and working as a professional writer—that Labrie turned to painting. She had always been interested in art, but an unfortunate incident as a teenager had somewhat soured her on the field: she had been transferred out of an art class for refusing to follow the rules of academic art. She remains a confirmed radical. The favored elements in her paintings—such as a horse, child, or tree—tower over the rest of the composition, violating all rules of proportion; colors glow and clash with no regard for the rules of nature. She knows only one rule—her immediate feelings about the subject matter and how she feels it should be rendered.

Labrie's techniques and her attitude toward her material have changed somewhat with time. She now paints not only rural New England landscapes but also interiors, portraits, ships, and genre paintings. She works in oils on canvas, but she no longer—as she once did—tries to dry paintings by putting them in the oven! She has become something of a cult figure, with her paintings appearing on the covers of such publications as *Early American Life.* She has even designed a painting for use with needlepoint kits.

Rose Labrie lives and works in Portsmouth, New Hampshire. Her paintings have been exhibited at Strawberry Banke Colonial Preservation, Portsmouth, New Hampshire; the Palm Beach Galleries, Palm Beach, Florida; the Shayne Gallery, Montreal, Canada; and the Ogunquit Gallery, Ogunquit, Maine, among others.

Rose Labrie
*King, the Leprechaun Pony*
1982
Oil on canvas; 16″ x 20″
Private collection

Rose Labrie
*On a Sunday Afternoon*
1977
Oil on canvas; 30″ x 40″
Collection of Dr. Robert
Bishop

# Sol Landau

Sol Landau's sculpture has been greatly influenced by his childhood on New York City's Lower East Side. Born in New York in 1919, he has remained a lifelong resident and has been an active member of the Jewish community from which he draws much of his inspiration.

As a child, Landau worked with clay; as an adult, he whittled; but it was not until his retirement from the New York Department of Parks that he turned to carving as a full-time activity. Classes at the Brooklyn Museum Art School in 1976 sharpened his skills, but he remains essentially unschooled.

Landau's sculpture grows out of his experience in a close-knit Jewish family and neighborhood. Works like *The Rabbi* evoke community traditions, while more personal examples, such as *Memories*—in which a housewife pauses in her labors to look wistfully at a family photograph—call to mind the births, departures, and deaths that are part of all human existence. That Landau can capture in sculptured forms such fleeting passions and expressions tells much of the quality and depth of his work.

The artist's work tells much about the artist. He has always felt himself to be shy and somewhat introverted, and his figures reflect this, enabling him, as he sees it, to bring out "a lot of feelings I couldn't express in words." But he also has a close family life, and this is reflected in his group sculptures.

Landau's figures are sculpted from softwood, usually pine or bass. Bodies are modeled in a single piece, limbs are done separately then doweled or glued to the body. The figures are then painted with acrylics. Many are mounted on bases that accommodate other elements of the composition, such as desks, tables, and chests. The broad, flat faces have an almost totemic quality, quite in contrast to the seemingly mundane tasks the figures are often performing—but the tasks are often as much symbolic as functional.

The work of Sol Landau is included in the permanent collection of the John Judkyn Memorial, Freshford Manor, Bath, England, and has been exhibited at the Shirley Stuart Gallery, Southampton, New York, and at the offices of the American Hebrew Congregationalists, New York City.

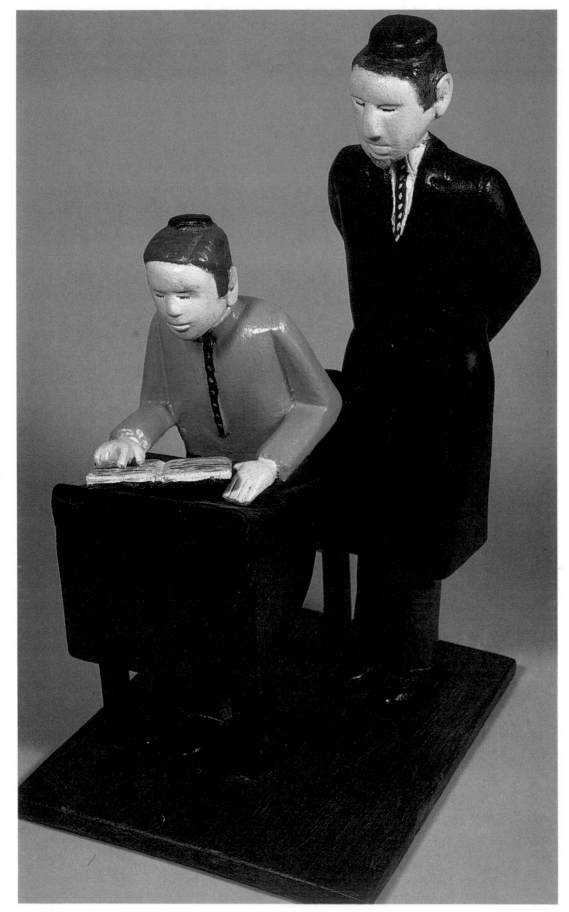

Sol Landau
*The Rabbi*
1981
Carved and painted wood;
28″ high
Collection of Isobel and
Harvey Kahn
Photo by Bill Buckner

*Opposite:* Sol Landau
*Memories*
1981
Carved and painted wood;
30″ high
Collection of Mr. and Mrs.
Robert Marcus
Photo by Bill Buckner

Sol Landau
*Feeding the Cat*
1982
Carved and painted wood;
26" high
Private collection
Photo by Bill Buckner

# Tom Langan

The work of Tom Langan evolves directly out of the American tradition of decoy making, the carving of wooden representations of ducks, geese, and swans that are used to lure game birds to within range of hunters' guns. Born on New York's Long Island, Langan grew up observing and admiring the waterfowl and small animals that abounded along the shores and in the woods. In his early teens he began to carve decoys. He traded or sold the decoys to fellow hunters, and by the mid 1970s some of these pieces had begun to appear in antiques shops, often listed as being much older than they actually were.

Alarmed at this, Langan began to sign and sometimes date his work. He discovered that he had a much wider audience than he had thought; not only hunters, but also collectors of folk art wanted to own his creations. As his own interests and his following expanded, Langan began to carve other things than waterfowl. Weathervanes, fish carvings, and, finally, mythical beasts such as the fabled unicorn entered his repertoire. Today, he produces dozens of highly varied carvings each year.

Langan's work has attracted critical attention for its skillful combination of characterization and anatomical exactness. His pieces have a reality about them that transcends life. They are frequently taken for much older work because Langan likes to use ancient cracked and checked pieces of pine or cedar, to apply metal braces that simulate repair, and to artificially age his paints. The net effect is that of an assumed antiquity.

Works by Tom Langan are in the permanent collection of the Museum of American Folk Art, and they have been exhibited both there and at the Nassau County Fine Arts Museum in Roslyn, New York.

Tom Langan
*Swans*
ca. 1970
Carved and painted wood;
43″ x 25″
Private collection

Tom Langan
*Unicorn*
ca. 1975
Carved and painted wood;
48″ x 33″ x 11″
Private collection

# Lawrence Lebduska

One of the first 20th-century American folk artists to gain some measure of recognition, Lawrence Lebduska was born in Baltimore, Maryland, in 1894. His family was from Bohemia, an area of western Czechoslovakia. When they returned there temporarily during the early 1900s, Lawrence learned both decorating and the art of making stained glass, a trade followed by his father. After the family came back to the United States in 1912, he became a decorative mural painter and also began to spend his spare time painting scenes that pleased him.

Although he did not take lessons and appears to have avoided museums and academic art, some aspects of Lebduska's work, particularly its bold colors, resembled that of the Fauvists, a group of experimental French painters active about the time Lebduska was studying in Europe. His paintings made a great impact during the 1930s. According to some accounts, they were the inspiration that led the wealthy Abby Aldrich Rockefeller to assemble her important collection of American folk art. Unfortunately, the popularity of Lebduska's works lacked the almost universal nature it now possesses, and by the 1940s Lebduska was largely forgotten. With the renewed interest in folk art during the 1960s, Lebduska was once more in fashion, but he had little time to enjoy it. He died in 1966.

Lebduska's paintings vary widely in subject matter, from the animal scenes like *Frolicking Horses*; to portraits, often of collectors who had befriended him; to complex pseudohistorical compositions such as *Land of the Pease (sic)*. His more fanciful themes were taken from fairy tales, particularly Czechoslovakian legends, from childhood memories, and even from such mundane sources as books he had read, postcards he had received, and children's books he browsed through. Lebduska worked in various mediums, including oil on canvas and pastel on paper.

Lawrence Lebduska
*Horses at Play*
1965
Oil on canvas; 24″ x 36″
Collection of Gary Davenport
Photo by Bill Buckner

# Abraham Levin

Born near Vilna, Lithuania, in 1880, Abraham Levin came to the United States in 1903 and, along with thousands of other immigrant Jews, went to work in New York City's garment industry. For nearly thirty-five years, he toiled in the sweat-shops of Manhattan, stitching together boys' pants in a dark, crowded room filled with sewing machines and other workers.

Beneath his surface acquiescence in the "system" burned a fierce resentment and a desire to express himself—to tell his story and the story of his people. At the age of fifty-seven, Levin left the sewing rooms and began to paint. At first he worked only in pen and ink, but in time he turned to oils. His subject matter was his life, from the ghettos and the fields of eastern Europe that he remembered from his childhood to the tenements, shops, synagogues, and streets of New York City's Lower East Side.

Some critics have compared Levin's paintings to those of Chagall, perceiving in them the same otherworldly, dreamlike quality. The comparison may be valid on a superficial level, but Levin's work is clearly of a darker order. His subjects are clad in somber shades and writhe in torment. The face of a worker crouched over a sewing machine shows sheer exhaustion. Three figures facing a table full of food look beyond it into a future that seems to offer them little sustenance, physical or spiritual.

There can be no doubt that Levin's works came from his heart. As he once said, "I paint entirely from memory. I am satisfied because I express myself. . . . I paint my own little town, my people, my own life from my youth to this moment." It is clear that Levin saw the life of the working class as hard, but while he labored to improve its lot through unions and political activity, in the long run, it was his painting that made the most lasting impression.

Abraham Levin's paintings are in various collections and have been exhibited publicly both here, where they formed part of a traveling show organized by the Smithsonian Institution, and abroad, where they were shown in the First Triennial of Insitic Art at Bratislava, Czechoslovakia, in 1966.

Abraham Levin
*Woman with Still Life*
1940
Oil on Masonite; 30" x 36"
Jay Johnson America's Folk
Heritage Gallery
Photo by Bill Buckner

Abraham Levin
*The Tailor*
1940–47
Oil on canvas; 22″ x 28″
Collection of Dr. Robert
Bishop
Photo by Bill Buckner

Abraham Levin
*Sharing Bread and Wine*
1940–47
Oil on canvas; 22″ x 28″
Collection of Rubens Teles
Photo by Bill Buckner

# Harry Lieberman

Nearly thirty years would be regarded as a lengthy career for most artists, but for Harry Lieberman it was only a portion of a life that spanned a century. Born in Gnieveshev, Poland, in 1877, Lieberman came to this country in 1906 and went to work as a cutter in the garment trade. He later became a candy manufacturer, finally retiring in his late seventies. As with several other contemporary folk artists, he joined a senior citizen's organization, and this affiliation led to a new career. When his regular chess partner failed to appear one day, Lieberman decided to spend the day in a painting class. He was so delighted with the new experience that he immediately began to paint.

Lieberman had studied to be a rabbi during his youth in Poland, and his work reflects his knowledge of the Old Testament, the Cabala, and the Talmud. Typical of these paintings is *Children's Children Are the Crown of Old Men, and the Adornment of Children Are Their Fathers*, a touching study of a grandfather, father, and son studying the Talmud together. As in much of Lieberman's work, the central figures in this painting are set against a complex, tapestrylike background. His paintings are also characterized by a delicate filigree work employed for trees and bushes. It is likely that both the complex backgrounds and the filigree work can be traced to Lieberman's years handling textiles in the garment industry.

The painting classes he took had little effect on Lieberman's style. A conversation he had with Larry Rivers, an important contemporary academic artist who was for a brief time the instructor of a class of which Lieberman was a member, is particularly instructive. After several classes, Lieberman became aware that Rivers was helping other students but ignoring him. When he asked Rivers why, the instructor replied, "I can't teach you more than what you are already doing. . . . What you do is right the way it is." Few academic artists have shown such good judgment!

Harry Lieberman lived and worked in Great Neck, New York, until his death at age 106 in 1983.

Harry Lieberman
*Children's Children Are the Crown of Old Men, and the Adornment of Children Are Their Fathers*
1977
Oil on canvas paper; 14" x 18"
Private collection
Photo by Bill Buckner

*Following page:*
Harry Lieberman
*9 AM Bar Mitzvah*
1972
Oil on paper; 16" x 20"
Collection of Herbert W. Hemphill, Jr.

# The Lopez Family

Felix A. Lopez
*San Ysidro*
1982
Wood polychrome; 36" x 47"
Collection of Mr. and Mrs.
Gerhard Stebich

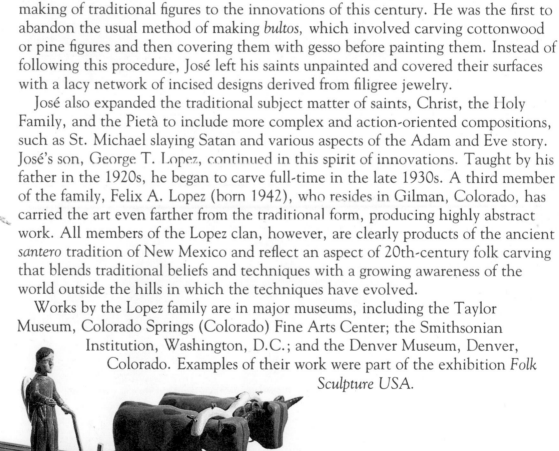

Six generations of the Lopez family of Cordoba, New Mexico, have devoted themselves to a unique branch of American folk sculpture: the carving of the religious figures known as *bultos*. Known as *santeros*, or "makers of saints," certain artists of New Mexico and southern Colorado have produced pictures *(retablos)* and carvings *(bultos)* for over two hundred years to adorn the churches and house shrines of southwestern Spanish-American communities.

Although the craft died out in the late 19th century, a few artists continued to work, and among the best known of these are the members of the Lopez family. The most prominent, José Dolores Lopez (1868–1938), spanned the era from the making of traditional figures to the innovations of this century. He was the first to abandon the usual method of making *bultos*, which involved carving cottonwood or pine figures and then covering them with gesso before painting them. Instead of following this procedure, José left his saints unpainted and covered their surfaces with a lacy network of incised designs derived from filigree jewelry.

José also expanded the traditional subject matter of saints, Christ, the Holy Family, and the Pietà to include more complex and action-oriented compositions, such as St. Michael slaying Satan and various aspects of the Adam and Eve story. José's son, George T. Lopez, continued in this spirit of innovations. Taught by his father in the 1920s, he began to carve full-time in the late 1930s. A third member of the family, Felix A. Lopez (born 1942), who resides in Gilman, Colorado, has carried the art even farther from the traditional form, producing highly abstract work. All members of the Lopez clan, however, are clearly products of the ancient *santero* tradition of New Mexico and reflect an aspect of 20th-century folk carving that blends traditional beliefs and techniques with a growing awareness of the world outside the hills in which the techniques have evolved.

Works by the Lopez family are in major museums, including the Taylor Museum, Colorado Springs (Colorado) Fine Arts Center; the Smithsonian Institution, Washington, D.C.; and the Denver Museum, Denver, Colorado. Examples of their work were part of the exhibition *Folk Sculpture USA*.

José Dolores Lopez
*Nuestra Señora de la Luz*
1936
Carved cottonwood; 40″
high
Taylor Museum, Colorado
Springs Fine Arts Center

*Opposite:* George T. Lopez
*Adam and Eve*
1965
Carved wood; 13½″ x 11½″
Collection of Rubens Teles

# George Edwin Lothrop

It is often the fate of artists, both folk and academic, to be unappreciated in their lifetimes. Such was the case with George Edwin Lothrop. Born in Dighton, Massachusetts, in 1867, Lothrop was trained as a piano-case carver and worked at this trade and as a watchman and doorkeeper. But these were merely ways to earn a living: Lothrop's real ambitions were much higher. He was simultaneously a painter, playwright, poet, and would-be actor. He is known to have written and published—at his own expense—over one dozen plays, one hundred fifty poems, and a collection of sheet music. He also invented a motion-picture device, "revolutionizing the business, improving the films 200 percent."

Regrettably, no one showed much interest in Lothrop's writing; his paintings drew only slightly more notice. Although his work was accepted for the exhibitions of the Society of Independent Artists from 1917 to 1920, it appears to have attracted neither attention nor buyers in the artist's lifetime. When Lothrop died in 1939 of a stroke suffered on a Boston street, he was destitute and had not worked for many years.

Some years after the artist's death, a group of his paintings were found in storage and offered for sale through a thrift shop. These oils on canvas ultimately attracted the attention of folk art collectors. Many of them were embellished with costume jewelry in the manner of a collage. The subject matter of the paintings reflects the artist's interest in the theater, music, and 19th-century literature. A work such as *The Muses* combines a classical theme and bold colors with Lothrop's penchant for painting the undraped female form. The faces in these works are reminiscent of those painted by the academic artist James Ensor; the jewellike quality of the details calls to mind Persian miniatures. While it is possible that Lothrop may have been familiar with academic painting, his treatment of the subject matter is hardly academic. Arbitrary scale, nonnatural color schemes, and highly personal composition mark his pieces as unique.

George Lothrop worked for the better part of two decades but left a relatively small number of paintings. These are in various private collections and have been exhibited on numerous occasions, including in the exhibition *Paintings by Two New England Primitives, J. O. J. Frost and George E. Lothrop,* at the Institute of Contemporary Art, Boston.

George Edwin Lothrop
*The Muses*
1928
Oil on canvas; 13¾″ x 22½″
Collection of Mr. and Mrs.
Elias Getz

# Emily Lunde

Emily Lunde was born in 1914 on a farm in the tiny northern Minnesota town of Newfolden. She has lived in Grand Forks, North Dakota, since 1942. A painter, Lunde takes as her subject matter the lives and activities of the Scandinavian immigrants who came to the Northwest during the early 1900s. Growing up with grandparents who could not yet speak English, Lunde was emersed in a culture that strongly reflected the customs of Sweden and Norway. The impressions she absorbed as a youth now fuel her creative imagination.

Though she was always interested in art, Lunde did not begin to paint until the 1950s. In part, this delay was due to the lack of free time in a life devoted to raising a family. However, the delay also reflected the lack of encouragement she received from those closest to her. Even today, with several exhibitions behind her and considerable recognition in the art world, Lunde remains largely unappreciated in her own community. As she once remarked, "They say the Apostles were not known in their own country, and it's true around here."

Lunde's work focuses not only on an area and a culture but on a period—the 1920s and 1930s, the years when she was growing up. In a sense, her work is more documentary than that of most memory painters. She remembers how it was and honestly reproduces it. Her works do not present a sanitized version of the past. Thus, she does not hesitate to depict the cruelty to animals and the prejudice against outsiders that existed in her area.

Lunde's paintings are primarily oils on Masonite or canvas. She works boldly, applying her colors with a supreme confidence but with a concern for realism that is often absent in this field. Genre topics are most common—stacking hay, knitting, a country carnival, a christening—all of them reflections of the life she lived.

Emily Lunde's work was shown at the University of North Dakota Art Gallery as part of the exhibition *Common Wealth: North Dakota Folk Art.* Her paintings are owned by, among others, the New York State Historical Society at Cooperstown and Mrs. Betty Ford.

Emily Lunde
*Wedding Party*
1978
Oil on canvas; 24" x 30"
Private collection

Emily Lunde
*Carnival Impressions*
1976
Oil on canvas; 24″ x 30″
Private collection

# Laura Lynch

Although she works in other mediums, too, Laura Lynch is best known for her remarkable appliquéd pictures, most of which depict the urban life that she sees in the streets of New York City. These quiltlike works, which are sometimes as large as eight feet by ten feet, are composed of carefully cut and stitched together bits of silk, corduroy, velvet, and various cottons. All of her pictures have a panoramic quality. A view of the beach at Oak Street, Chicago, encompasses not only the crowds milling about on the sand but the busy parkway fronting the park and a seemingly boundless sky and water, featuring bathers, boats, and even a plane towing a banner on which appear the artist's name and the date.

Lynch's incredibly whimsical *View from Maggie's Window* offers a vista of an apartment house that becomes a small world with such diverse open-window views as sleepers complete with dream pictures; an alligator in a bathtub; and a girl letting down her hair in the best fairy-tale fashion so that her prince can climb up it. Her *Washington Square Park* depicts the park just as New Yorkers would like it to be: filled with strolling musicians and happy people—no drug dealers, dirt, or derelicts.

The artist makes no apologies for the fact that her work is somewhat unrealistic. It grows out of her life and the way she views things. Inevitably, her works must reflect her personal vision, for she lives with them for a long time. Lynch takes six to twelve months to complete a picture, often carrying individual elements around with her so that she can work on them wherever she goes. She follows no set work schedule. As she says, "When I work, I work seven days a week; but when I rest, I rest." Born in Chicago in 1949, she now lives in the SoHo area of New York City.

The works of Laura Lynch have been exhibited at several galleries, including the Jay Horowitz Gallery in Chicago and the Allan Stone Gallery in New York City. Her works were included in a folk art exhibition at the Nassau County Fine Arts Museum, in Roslyn, New York.

Laura Lynch
*Washington Square Park*
1978
Felt, velvet, and corduroy appliqué wall hanging; 94″ x 76″
Collection of Mr. and Mrs. Robert Marcus

*Right:* Laura Lynch
*Oak Street Beach*
1976
Felt, velvet, and corduroy appliqué wall hanging; 84″ x 100″
Collection of Mr. and Mrs. Robert Marcus

# Justin McCarthy

Justin McCarthy was one of this century's most prolific and most complex folk artists. During his long career—he is known to have worked from the 1920s into the early 1970s—he produced hundreds of drawings and paintings on a bewildering variety of materials: oils on Masonite, board, canvas, and even tile; acrylics; watercolors; and crayon sketches. He painted everything from powerful abstract renditions of Washington crossing the Delaware to detailed representations of the animals, fruits, vegetables, and flowers he worked with at his rural home.

McCarthy was born in Weatherly, Pennsylvania, in 1891, the son of a well-to-do newspaperman and stock speculator. He grew up in a prosperous family that was cursed with misfortunes: the death of a favored younger brother was followed in 1908 by his father's demise. Bearing the burdens of his father's unfulfilled expectations, McCarthy flunked out of the University of Pennsylvania Law School and suffered a nervous breakdown a few years later. From 1915 to 1920, he was confined to a mental institution, and it was during this period that he began to paint.

Following his release, McCarthy settled with his mother at the family home in Weatherly, supporting himself by growing and selling vegetables and, in later years, by taking menial jobs. He worked constantly throughout this period, first at drawings and then, after his mother's death in 1940, in oils. Though he exhibited his work at county fairs, it remained unappreciated until 1960, when McCarthy was discovered by the artist Sterling Strausser. Thereafter, until his death in 1977, his reputation grew, with his works appearing in the galleries of the Metropolitan Museum of Art, the Museum of Modern Art, and the Museum of American Folk Art.

McCarthy's work is characterized by asymmetrical composition, exaggerated drawing featuring an intense line, and highly nonnaturalistic coloring. Because he worked in several different styles at the same time, it is possible to find pieces that are radically different even though they date from the same period. He remains one of the giants and enigmas of American folk art.

Justin McCarthy
*Marilyn Monroe*
ca. 1960
Oil on board; 22" x 28"
Collection of Mr. and Mrs.
Maurice C. Thompson, Jr.

Justin McCarthy
*George Washington Crossing
the Delaware*
1963
Oil on Masonite; 29½″ x 40″
Collection of Mr. and Mrs.
Gerhard Stebich

# Bryan McNutt

The carver Bryan McNutt produces remarkably whimsical flat-painted cutouts made primarily from pine that is painted and sometimes decorated with metal, glass, and other materials. His dedication to his work is unswerving. He often works twelve hours a day and has characterized himself as having an "uncontrollable urge to create things."

Little in McNutt's early life indicated that he would take the course he has taken. Born in Phillips, Texas, in 1942, he was bred to the range, and for twelve years he served as foreman of the Alan Ladd Ranch in California. When the ranch was sold, he decided to return to Texas and to seek employment as a carpenter. Dissatisfied with local wage scales, he began to work on his own, producing a group of coatracks in the shape of animals. When, somewhat to McNutt's surprise, these sold, he began to expand his activities. At first most of the carvings were utilitarian, but he gradually moved into the area of pure sculpture and went from a concentration on animals—of which he is very fond—to portraiture.

McNutt's figures have a startlingly lifelike aspect. Their eyes stare at you, wide-eyed with wonder. Their smiles are infectious; their permanents, permanent. Few of these portraits are taken from life; they reflect the memory and the great good humor of their creator.

McNutt lives and works in Collegville, Texas. He carves in a garage where, as he describes it, "I freeze in the winter and die in the summer." His works have been exhibited at the Museum of International Folk Art, Santa Fe, New Mexico, and at the Dallas (Texas) State Fair; illustrated articles on his carvings have appeared in the Fort Worth *Star Telegram*.

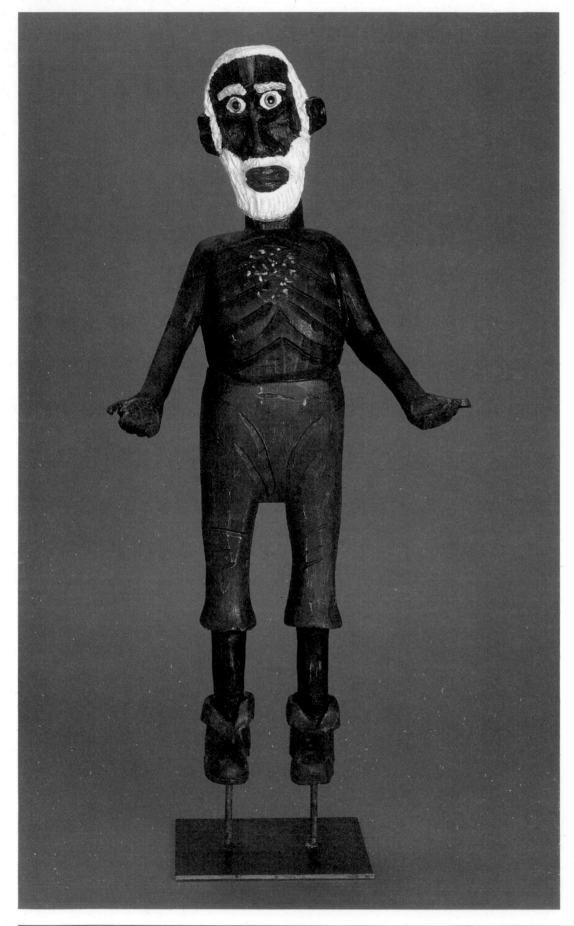

Bryan McNutt
*The Old Man*
1982
Carved and painted wood;
21½″ high
Collection of Dr. Robert
Bishop

*Opposite:* Bryan McNutt
*Blonde*
1983
Carved and painted wood;
16″ high
Private collection

# David George Marshall

Some thirty years ago, while working as a surveyor's assistant, Dave Marshall in an idle moment scratched out a face on a water-smoothed rock he found in a creek bed. Pleased by the result, he began to experiment with sculptural forms. Today, Marshall carves individuals and groups from soft, water-rounded rocks.

Marshall describes his creative process as follows:

After almost thirty years of walking creeks and collecting, there are certain things I look for. The amount of water a rock retains when it is partly submerged is very important. Suitable stones for carving with knives are few and far between. I soak the stones in several garbage cans of water to keep them prepared for carving. In the winter I add salt and antifreeze to the water. Generally, the shape of the stone influences the shape of the figure I carve. Detail and subject matter come to me as I carve.

Using more than forty different carving knives, Marshall shapes the stones to a generally rounded conformation with interesting details, such as neckties, buttons, and facial features, carefully incised into the surface. Admitting to a generally pessimistic outlook on life, he is always somewhat surprised to see that many of his figures turn out to appear quite cheerful. Others, however, seem to bear the weight of the world on their sagging shoulders. These, oddly enough, are often products of days when Marshall himself is feeling rather cheerful.

Born in Nassau County, New York, in 1936, Marshall spent his childhood first in Virginia and then near Kingston, New York, where at the age of sixteen he left school to become a field hand. Thereafter, he worked off and on as paperhanger, painter, dairy-farm laborer, mink farmer, and factory hand, and put in several years in the U.S. Navy. He lives and works in Godeffrey, New York. His sculpture has been shown in New York City at the Jay Johnson America's Folk Heritage Gallery and at Aarne Anton's Gallery. Numerous pieces are in private collections.

David George Marshall
*Face*
not dated
Carved and painted creek-
stone; 8″ high
Collection of Lenny Kislin
Photo by Bill Buckner

David George Marshall
*Old Couple*
1980
Carved creekstone; 10″ high
Private collection
Photo by Bill Buckner

David George Marshall
*Funeral*
1982
Carved creekstone; 18″ x
7½″
Jay Johnson America's Folk
Heritage Gallery
Photo by Bill Buckner

# Ralph Middleton

During the 19th century, itinerant folk artists were the rule; today, they are the exception. Ralph Middleton, a black artist who roams the streets of New York City, painting in public and selling his works to passersby, is an example of this current minority, an itinerant artist. Since he is unwilling to reveal information about himself and will not disclose his age or place of residence, Middleton remains a mystery even to those who own his work.

Middleton has stated that he was born in and has always lived in Manhattan; that he was first inspired to paint at the age of sixteen when he visited several city museums; and that he has a wife and two children. Although he remains silent about the rest of his personal life, he is quite willing to talk about his philosophy of art. He says that he paints what he feels and that through his work he tries to "take the wrappings off of society"; he paints what he thinks is "really there."

Middleton employs a variety of media: he works in oils, acrylics, pen, pencil, and crayon, often combining several materials in the same work and preferring cardboard, paper, or Masonite as a surface. Subject matter varies but is primarily concerned with portraits or groups of people. Figures are exaggerated, particularly sexual characteristics, and there is a harshness both of color and line that is reminiscent of the German Expressionist movement of the 1920s. Unlike many folk artists, Middleton is unconcerned with detail. Overall impression and impact is his goal, and his subjects often have an agonized or frantic appearance that may reflect either the artist's state of mind or the milieu in which he works.

Ralph Middleton
*Portrait of a Man*
1980
Poster paint and pencil on
paper; 14″ x 22″
Collection of Rubens Teles

Ralph Middleton
*Naked Man*
1979
Poster paint and pencil on
paper; 14″ x 22″
Collection of Dr. Robert
Bishop

# Pamela Miles

Born in Oak Park, Illinois, in 1939, Pamela Miles now lives with her husband and children in Anchorage, Kentucky. She began to paint soon after she was married. At first she copied folk paintings pictured in books. Then, encouraged by her husband's mother, she began to idealize her paintings, to make them more her and less the source. Today, she uses old prints, photographs, and advertising materials to create still lifes and landscapes with her own distinct characteristics.

One of the most notable of these characteristics and one that endears Miles to her followers is the sharp focus that she gives to flowers and trees. Her "flower paintings," as she calls them, are among her most popular works. Flowers by Pamela Miles seem almost to jump off the canvas. The source of her inspiration in this work is her observation of color changes and atmospheric effects in nature, phenomena that she translates to canvas. The glowing vitality of a Miles canvas may be hard to describe, but once seen it is not easily forgotten.

Miles works in acrylic on canvas or plywood. She has no set painting schedule but tends to work when the house is quiet and during summer or when her husband is away on business.

Paintings by Pamela Miles are in various private collections and have been widely shown. Among the galleries that have displayed her work are the Swearingen Gallery, Louisville, Kentucky; The Abby, Lake Geneva, Wisconsin; and the Arts Exclusive Gallery, Simsbury, Connecticut.

Pamela Miles
*Pennsylvania Dutch Bouquet*
1982
Acrylic on canvas; 34″ x 36″
Collection of the artist

Pamela Miles
*Spring Plowing*
1980
Oil on canvas; 30″ x 40″
Collection of
Anthony Petullo

# Peter Minchell

The folk artist Peter Minchell was born in Treves, Germany, in 1889. After attending a trade school there at the turn of the century, he immigrated to New Orleans in 1906. After several years in Louisiana, Minchell settled in Florida in 1911 and entered the building trade, a pursuit he followed until retirement in the late 1950s.

Though it is not certain when Minchell began to paint, by 1960 he had begun to produce remarkable floral compositions featuring incredibly lush flowers and trees whose colors and composition had a strange, unworldly quality. In 1972, he began his Geological Phenomena series, a group of paintings illustrating dramatic and oftimes frightening natural elements, such as hurricanes, tornadoes, and tidal waves. This was the first of several series or groups devoted to specific subjects such as "the end of the earth," space visitors, and similar unusual subjects.

Minchell works in watercolor on paper. His carefully detailed paintings are often accompanied by an explanatory "story" written in extremely tiny script at the foot of the work. Though certain elements of the present and of the artist's past intrude, these paintings are almost pure fantasy, reflecting Minchell's extraordinary imagination and the highly introspective nature that fuels his very personal vision.

The watercolors of Peter Minchell are in various public and private collections.

Peter Minchell
*The Virtuous Genes from
Planet Earth*
not dated
Watercolor on paper;
20″ x 26″
Collection of Herbert W.
Hemphill, Jr.

# Barbara Moment

Born in rural Easton, Pennsylvania, around 1930, and growing up surrounded by chickens, cows, and other domesticated animals, Barbara Moment has developed into one of the most innovative folk painters. Her works are usually of sheep, pigs, or cows, but they are set in landscapes filled with a Rousseau-like mystery. A ram watches as a line of ewes passes behind him against a background of dark and brooding trees while overhead the moon rises against a black sky; set far back in the woods is a monument in the form of yet another ewe. In another painting, two merino sheep pause in an otherwise strangely empty landscape. All is shades of green, and a pestilential sun glows down from above. These are not just pretty paintings of lovely animals. The animals have character and perceptible intentions —not always the best of intentions.

Barbara Moment lives in South Nyack, New York, with her painter husband. Originally a writer who liked to paint, the unexpected sale at a local art show of one of her works led her to become in recent years an artist who likes to write. She works in the family dining room on a fairly regular schedule and now prefers acrylics on canvas or wood, though at an earlier stage she worked in oils. Her animal paintings reflect not only her love of animals and her experience with them but also keen observation of the woodcuts and lithographs of domestic stock used to illustrate 19th- and early 20th-century farm manuals and almanacs.

Moment's paintings were exhibited as part of the *Folk, Fantasy & Expressionism* show at the Silvermine Guild Center for the Arts, New Canaan, Connecticut, and have also been shown at the Mulvane Art Center, Topeka, Kansas, and at special exhibitions at Bloomingdale's, New York, and Marshall Field, Chicago. *House Beautiful* and *American Home* magazines have both featured her work.

Barbara Moment
*Two Sheep*
1983
Oil on canvas; 20″ x 24″
Collection of Dr. and Mrs. David Bronstein

Barbara Moment
*Farmer Noah*
1983
Oil on canvas; 30″ x 40″
Private collection

# Sister Gertrude Morgan

The powerful motivating effect of religious conviction on some folk artists is clearly illustrated in the life of Gertrude Morgan. Born in Lafayette, Alabama, in 1900, Morgan was always deeply religious and at the age of thirty-seven became an evangelist. Two years later, she settled in New Orleans, where she became a street preacher for a fundamentalist sect, started an orphanage, and built a small church.

In 1956, Morgan began to paint. A year later, in response to what she perceived to be a "divine word," she began to dress entirely in white and to create for herself an all-white environment: furniture, window shades, fans, even the case in which she carried her guitar. In a sense, Morgan was a forerunner of the conceptualist artists of the 1960s, creating an environment that became art.

After her orphanage was destroyed by a hurricane in 1965, she began to concentrate on painting, working in pen and pencil and oil and acrylics on paper, cardboard, or canvas. Morgan had always painted. She once said, "When I was a little girl, I was always trying to draw something. I used to draw on the ground with a stick." Her adult work was clearly associated with her religious beliefs. Not only was the subject matter generally inspired by biblical teachings, but the artist felt herself divinely inspired, claiming that, "He moves my hand. Do you think I would ever know how to do a picture like this by myself?"

As with many folk artists who choose a religious subject matter, Morgan combined pictorial representation with calligraphy, using the written word to illustrate and expand upon the themes of her paintings. Such works are teaching tools, and it is clear that even those of her paintings that are autobiographical are designed to encourage and instruct the faithful.

The paintings of Sister Gertrude Morgan have been widely exhibited. Among the institutions at which they have been shown are the Museum of American Folk Art, New York City; Louisiana State University; the La Jolla Museum of Contemporary Art in California; and Virginia Commonwealth University at Richmond.

Sister Gertrude Morgan
*Modern Inventions*
1970
Oil on cardboard; 14″ x 18″
Collection of Dr. Robert Bishop

*Opposite:* Sister Gertrude
Morgan
*Untitled*
1970
Tempera and pen on paper;
29″ x 24″
Collection of Herbert W.
Hemphill, Jr.

# Grandma Moses

The "mother of 20th-century folk art," Anna Mary Robertson Moses—or Grandma Moses, as she has become known to several generations of folk art enthusiasts—was born September 7, 1860, in Greenwich, New York. Much of her life was spent in eastern New York State (she died in 1961 in Hoosick Falls, close to the Vermont border) and in Virginia, where she lived the life of a conventional farm wife, sewing, tending children and domestic animals, doing the family wash, and attending the traditional rural social events—weddings, funerals, harvestings, and grange meetings.

Although she described herself as having been an avid artist as a child, it was not until she was in her seventies that Grandma Moses began to paint in earnest. Her first works, made as gifts for family and friends, reflected a blend of memories and her knowledge of popular prints such as those of Currier & Ives. From her memories she took interiors, activities, and the rolling fields and woodlands of eastern New York; from the prints, she took a sense of organization and the ability to render buildings and living creatures.

Moses's paintings might have remained unknown had not a New York City collector chanced upon several of them displayed in the window of a Hoosick Falls drugstore. Seized by the spontaneous quality and charming use of color in the paintings, he approached the artist. Moses's career began. In 1939, she broke into the public consciousness as one of seventeen *Contemporary Unknowns* featured in an exhibition for members at the Museum of Modern Art in New York City. The next year, she was given her first one-woman exhibition.

By the late 1940s, Grandma Moses was almost a household word, her popularity greatly enhanced by the exposure she received through reproductions of her paintings as postcards and on textiles. She continued to work throughout the 1950s, and as she grew older her style became more individual. Details became more abstract as she developed her own ideographic shorthand; drawing on her knowledge of embroidery, she learned to break forms down into their component colors, an almost impressionistic technique. Most of her later works were done in oils on canvas or board—her earlier efforts include works in house paint on cardboard.

Though many have envied her fame and some have derided her importance as a folk artist, Grandma Moses remains the pivotal figure in the 20th-century folk movement. Her universal appeal assured a far warmer welcome to later aspirants than they could ever have hoped for without her as a trailblazer.

Paintings by Grandma Moses are in most major museums, including the Metropolitan Museum of Art and the Museum of American Folk Art in New York City, and the Phillips Collection, Washington, D.C.

Grand
*The Di*
Copyri
Promis

*Vays*; 1947; oil on pressed wood; 16" x 20"
Grandma Moses Properties Co., New York
mory of Otto Kallir to the Museum of American Folk Art

# Janet Munro

Though she takes as her subject matter the landscapes and interiors of 19th-century New England, Janet Munro cannot be considered a memory painter—she is far too young to have experienced the scenes she paints. Born in 1949 in Woburn, Massachusetts, Janet Andrea Lehne Munro spent her childhood in rural Somerset County, New Jersey, marrying there and running a dairy farm before moving to her present home in Anna Maria Island, Florida.

Like most children, she liked to draw, but unlike most, she was strongly encouraged by a paternal grandmother who not only helped her to find her way artistically but also filled her with tales of life long ago. This, coupled with growing up in a home filled with antiques, caused Mrs. Munro—as she is known from the signature on her paintings—to develop an early affinity for the architecture and interiors of the northeastern United States. Her initial efforts, however, were portraits, and it was not until 1969 that she painted her first landscape. She didn't like it, but other people did, and since then she has worked steadily, often on a seven-days-a-week basis.

Janet Munro's paintings are characterized by great attention to detail, with even the smallest elements—such as the letters on an alphabet sampler seen on a distant wall or the clapboards on a partially obscured house—carefully delineated. Perspective may vary within a picture, offering the observer several different points of view, and Munro's colors often have a richness uncharacteristic of genre painters. She works in oils and egg tempera on wooden board and canvas, using photographs of the New England landscape, animals, houses, and events as models. Whatever the source of a figure or a concept might be, it eventually becomes part of the complex tapestry that is her work.

Janet Munro has achieved a high degree of success as an artist. Her paintings are in many collections, including those of the White House and the Smithsonian Institution, Washington, D.C.; individual owners include Dr. Benjamin Spock and Senator Edward Kennedy.

Janet Munro
*Making a Quilt*
1982
Oil on canvas; 18″ x 24″
Collection of Martin and
Lynne Klenert

Janet Munro
*Winter in Bar Harbor, Maine*
1982
Egg tempera on Masonite; 12″ x 24″
Collection of Rubens Teles

Janet Munro
*North Bay Street*
1982
Oil on Masonite; 23″ x 48″
Collection of Mr. and Mrs. James K. Sharp

# Virgil Norberg

Very few folk sculptors choose to work in metal, for it is both costly and difficult to handle. The remarkable cut-out sheet-metal weathervanes made by Virgil Norberg are almost unique in type and are certainly unique in inspiration. Born in Galesburg, Illinois, in 1930, Norberg grew up along the Rock River, an area then largely rural and quite traditional in outlook. Sundays were spent in church, and spare time was passed in the woods or along the waters, where great flocks of ducks and geese flew. This childhood hardly prepared Norberg for the worldly experiences of a brief naval career, but the contradictions that became evident to him have provided the foundation for a strong and viable art.

Religious themes predominate in his work, but traditional figures such as Adam and Eve and the grim reaper are treated in a variety of ways, ranging from a more-or-less recognizable Garden of Eden to a representation of Death as a machine gunner clad in a bold blue-and-red uniform. In all of Norberg's works, the flat planes of the cut sheet metal are emphasized by equally flat color application, and a general abstraction prevails.

Nominally weathervanes, these pieces are in reality sculpture in motion, and one wonders if Norberg did not choose the vane—a piece traditionally displayed outdoors, particularly on churches—as a means of reaching, at least symbolically, a larger audience.

While traditional in belief if not in artistic approach, Norberg proves equally traditional in his family life. Happily married, he lives with his family in Daven-

Virgil Norberg
*Jonah in the Whale*
1978
Sheet-metal weathervane;
67" x 67"
Collection of Richard and
Lois Rosenthal

Virgil Norberg
*Adam and Eve*
1979
Sheet-metal weathervane;
40″ x 48″
Private collection
Photo by Bill Buckner

port, Iowa, and holds a full-time job. He does his art in the mornings, evenings, and on weekends.

Virgil Norberg's works are owned by several museums, including the John Judkyn Memorial at Freshford Manor, Bath, England, and they have been displayed at, among others, the Evanston Art Center, Evanston, Illinois, the Central School of Art & Design, London, and the Bede Gallery, Jarrow, both in England. He was featured in the Iowa Arts Council exhibition *Passing Time and Traditions*.

Virgil Norberg
*Death*
Sheet-metal weathervane;
52″ x 33″
1978
Collection of Dr. Robert
Bishop

# James Joseph Nyeste

The folk potter James Joseph Nyeste creates elaborate and often humorous animals from the red clay of southern Pennsylvania. Born in Detroit, Michigan, in 1943, Nyeste lives and works on an 18th-century farm in Green Valley, Pennsylvania. He feels that his art is greatly influenced by the forms created at the 19th-century Bell Pottery in Waynesboro, Pennsylvania, and by the rich glazes employed by the folk potters who worked in the Shenandoah Valley of Virginia during the period 1850 to 1900.

It would be a mistake to assume that Nyeste is a mere copyist. His animals have a distinct character, one that reflects the individual talents of their creator. Nyeste takes shapes and motifs that appeared on such diverse objects as English Staffordshire china, American redware, and Pennsylvania Dutch chalkware and blends them to create new forms. A blissful cow crouches protectively over a basket of fruit; a cat—or is it a lion?—waits expectantly; a perky rooster stands guard. They are all charming and all distinctly different. Nyeste's ability to create rich, multi-colored glazes greatly enhances the charm of the figures. Rich greens, yellows, reds, browns, and blues flow over the bodies of the figures. No two pieces ever show the same color pattern.

There are few folk potters today, and the work of James Joseph Nyeste is unique among the craftsmen active in this field.

James Joseph Nyeste
*Old Tom*
1982
Glazed-redware sculpture;
7½" x 5" high
Private collection
Photo by Bill Buckner

James Joseph Nyeste
*Rooster*
1982
Glazed-redware sculpture;
5" high
Private collection
Photo by Bill Buckner

James Joseph Nyeste
*Cow with Basket*
1981
Glazed-redware sculpture;
6" high
Private collection
Photo by Bill Buckner

# Saturnino Portuondo "Pucho" Odio

One of the major folk carvers of this generation, Saturnino Portuondo Odio—
known to most collectors as "Pucho"—combines a childhood in a culture steeped
in folk art with a natural talent for wood carving. He was born in 1928 in Santiago
de Cuba and lived in Cuba until he was thirty-five, working at a variety of trades,
including those of carpenter, shoemaker, barber, and sailor. He came to this country in 1963 and worked here as a barber until 1974. Since then he has devoted
himself primarily to sculpture.

Like so many folk sculptors, Odio came well-equipped to his trade. Years of
handling wood and leather as a carpenter and shoemaker had made him familiar
with tools and with the properties of wood; barbering had taught him shaping and
proportions. It is small wonder, then, that Pucho's artistic tendencies were mani-
fested as a carver of wood.

Pucho is a man of the city—and of that most unusual of all cities, New York.
When he started to look for materials, he turned first to the streets and then to the
parks. Even today, most of his wood comes from Central Park.

Pucho's figures range in size from tiny animals no more than six inches high to
nearly full-size humans and animals. All are imbued with great charm and personality and not a little of the creator's own wonderful humor. Colors may be flat and
bold, as in the powerful blues and reds of a woman eating watermelon, or amazingly subtle, as in the spreading tail of a life-size peacock. Pucho's dogs and cats
are especially charming, reflecting a lifetime spent observing these traditional
domestic companions. Cats lick their fur or stare quizzically at imagined mice.
Dogs crouch alertly as though listening for familiar footfalls. All these
beings have a tremendous sense of life—the same life that courses
through the veins of their inspired creator.

Pucho Odio's work is now included in the permanent collections
of the Museum of American Folk Art in New York City and the
John Judkyn Memorial at Freshford Manor, Bath, England. His
pieces have been exhibited in various institutions, most recently
at the Mulvane Art Center, Topeka, Kansas, and the Nassau
County Fine Arts Museum, Roslyn, New York.

Saturnino Portuondo
"Pucho" Odio
*Hmm, It's Good*
1982
Carved and painted wood;
22″ high x 9″ wide
Collection of Lisa S. Roberts

*Opposite:* Saturnino Por-
tuondo "Pucho" Odio
*Black Cat*
1979
Carved and painted wood;
17½″ high
Jay Johnson America's Folk
Heritage Gallery
Photo by Bill Buckner

Saturnino Portuondo
"Pucho" Odio
*Peacock*
1982
Carved and painted wood;
45″ high x 53″ wide
Private collection
Photo by Bill Buckner

# Mattie Lou O'Kelley

Mattie Lou O'Kelley is the epitome of a folk artist—naive, reclusive, and tied to a rural background from which she draws her primary inspiration. The seventh of eight children born to a Georgia farm family, she spent her formative years on a hill farm in Banks County, working in the fields, sewing with her mother and sisters, assisting in the harvest and the canning of food, and experiencing all the joys and sorrows of a life that, even as she lived it, was an anachronism.

Her work reflects this background. The paintings—primarily landscapes and still lifes, although she has made a few interesting portraits—are highly symmetrical and tightly drawn with a great concern for detail, a quality that many enthusiasts find appealing. She works in oils on canvas. The themes—harvest, birth and death, local festivities, the simple pleasures of rural life—are closely related to those events celebrated in the nostalgic prints of Currier & Ives and *The Saturday Evening Post*. Like most folk artists, Mattie Lou denies outside influence, but it is evident that she has seen and recorded the bucolic renditions of American life that filled the pages of popular publications during the first half of this century.

Isolated from the mainstream of American life—she did not hold a job until she was thirty-five, she never married, and she has lived alone since her mother's death—she has developed a highly original style that includes a crude form of pointillism and a tapestrylike surface that lends a unifying air to works that are replete with detail.

Born in 1908, Mattie Lou did not begin to paint until 1950 and did not attract significant attention until the mid-1970s, but she has become one of the best known and most sought after of American folk painters. During the past few years, her work has been placed in major American collections, including those of the Museum of American Folk Art, New York City, the High Museum of Art, Atlanta, the Minneapolis Art Museum, and the Museum of International Folk Art, Santa Fe, New Mexico.

True to her character and background, the artist continues to paint in an environment very much like the one in which her work originated. After efforts to live in New York City and West Palm Beach, she has returned to Georgia and the simple life that she understands and expresses so well. Mattie Lou is also a poet. One of her poems, titled "Autobiography," ends:

Now my one room house has only me,
I never roam,
No lessons have I, but I paint
And paint
And stay at home.

Mattie Lou O'Kelley
*The Opossum Hunt*
1977
Oil on canvas; 36″ x 40″
Collection of Mr. and Mrs. Robert Marcus

Mattie Lou O'Kelley
*Snowy Day Around Town*
1978
Oil on canvas; 36″ x 48″
Collection of Mr. and Mrs. Edward C. Anderberg

Mattie Lou O'Kelley
*Fruit Time*
1981
Oil on canvas; 24" x 36"
Collection of Mr. and Mrs.
Robert Marcus
Photo by Bill Buckner

# Angela Palladino

Angela Palladino, born in 1929, is one of the few 20th-century folk artists whose work can be said to deal with feminist issues. A painter and sculptor, she came to the United States from her native Italy in 1958.

Palladino began to paint while hospitalized in London in 1965. She was bored, and her husband, noting that she had been sketching, brought her some materials. Within a short period, she was devoting most of her time to art.

Palladino works in acrylics on canvas and takes as her primary subject matter the role and state of the modern woman. She employs a narrative, or literary, style, often amplifying the visual image with accompanying text worked into the overall composition. Each picture becomes, in effect, a miniature melodrama illustrating some aspect of female existence. In *The Marriage Bureau,* for example, a group of painted photographs of somewhat ordinary but desperate-looking women is set against a green background, perhaps to represent a baize tabletop on which a potential suitor might display them.

In 1972, feeling the need for another outlet, Palladino began to sculpt in clay. She creates ghostly masks that are reminiscent of a Miró painting or the ritual masks made by the Eskimos of North America. Covered with simple, bright glazes and with the deep-set eyes and vacant looks of zombies, these masks evoke a very different world from that of Palladino's paintings.

The work of Angela Palladino has been exhibited at, among other places, the Merradin Gallery in London; the Rizzoli Gallery and the Museum of American Folk Art in New York City; the Cheekwood Museum in Nashville, Tennessee; the Akron Art Institute in Akron, Ohio; and the Columbus Museum of Arts and Sciences in Georgia. She received several awards at the Third International Biennale of Naive Art held at San Pellegrino, Italy, in 1978.

Angela Palladino
*The Happy Lady*
1975
Acrylic on canvas; 9″ x 12″
Collection of Eeva Inkeri

*Opposite:* Angela Palladino
*Lady with Tea Cup*
1966
Acrylic on canvas; 18″ x 21″
Collection of Alvin Grayson

# John Perates

John Perates was probably the most important religious carver of the 20th century. Born in Amphikleia, Greece, in 1895, Perates came to Portland, Maine, in 1912. He had been trained as a carver by his grandfather, and he went to work in Portland at a cabinet shop. In 1930, he was able to open his own business. At about the same time that he started his business, Perates began to create his life's work—a monumental series of relief carvings based on the life of Christ, including a pulpit, a bishop's throne, and an altar, all destined to be placed in the local Greek Orthodox church. The work seems to have been done in no particular order over a long period of time, occupying most of the years between 1930 and the sculptor's death in 1970.

Most of the work never found its way into the church. Some pieces, primarily panels, were used in the church, but most were considered too massive or too ostentatious and were relegated to the cellar—where they were discovered by an art historian.

Perates's carvings are strongly influenced by the traditional iconography of the Greek Orthodox church: they reflect the sculptor's familiarity with the religious icons, or representations of holy figures, customarily displayed in the churches of that denomination. However, Greek and Byzantine icons are traditionally made of metal or stone; Perates worked in wood. He favored hard timbers like maple, cherry, oak, or walnut, and his pieces were painted and varnished after carving.

Perates's sculpture also reflected his American experience. Not only did he favor the more subdued colors and natural wood tones of New England, but he also surrounded his primary figures with layers of concentric carving quite different from that found on European examples. The figures themselves are for the most part flattened frontal images with great power and presence, quite appropriate to their maker's declared purpose that they "represent the life of Christ from His baptism or spiritual birth to His death on the cross, those who wrote what He taught and those who carried on His teachings."

The work of John Perates has been exhibited throughout the United States and was taken to Japan for a special exhibition of American folk art from the Herbert W. Hemphill, Jr., Collection.

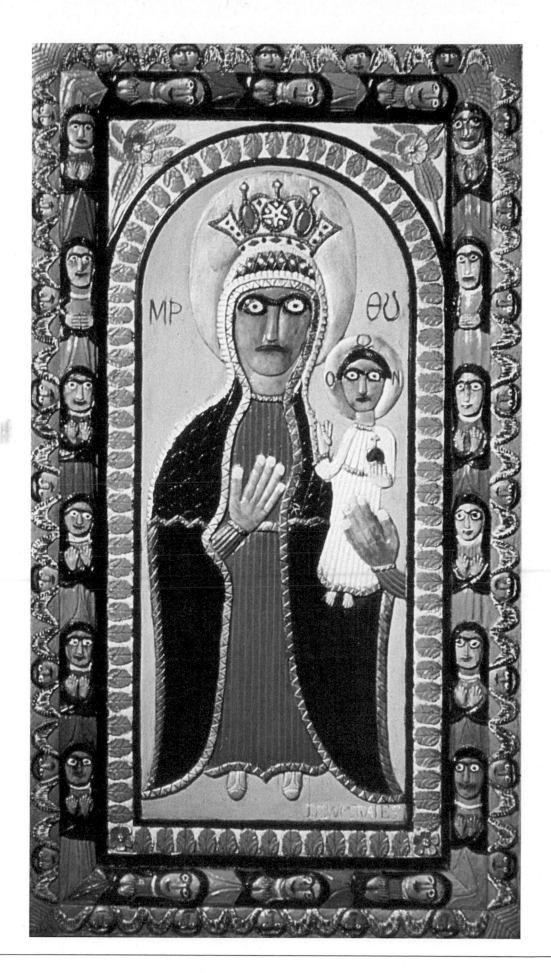

John Perates
*Madonna and Child*
1930–70
Carved and painted wood;
29″ x 20½″ x 3⅛″
Collection of Herbert W.
Hemphill, Jr.

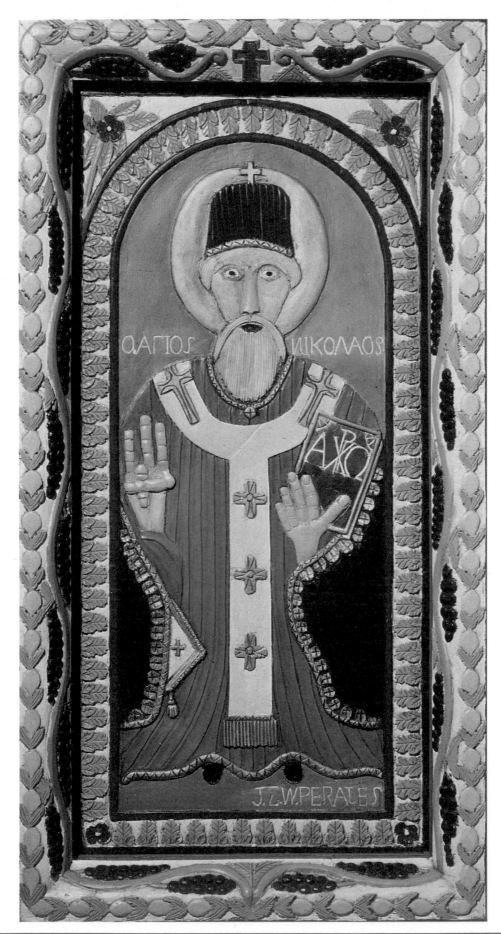

John Perates
*St. Nicholas*
1940
Carved and painted wood;
53″ high x 29″ wide
The Hall Collection of
American Folk and Isolate
Art

# The Painting Perkinses

As a family of folk painters, the Perkins clan is probably unique in the annals of 20th-century folk art. Mother, father, and daughter all paint, and although their styles vary, they all draw heavily on memories of rural Pennsylvania and Ohio, on simple religious beliefs, and on a view of the world that is charmingly naive.

The best known of the three, Ruth ("Ma") Perkins, started to paint in the late 1960s after she and her husband had retired from the management of the family restaurant, Ma Perkins' Chicken Inn. She displayed her work in an antiques shop that she owned, and in due course it was seen by a folk art collector. Scouting about for something to do in his spare time and impressed by his wife's sudden fame as an artist, Clarence ("Pa") Perkins took up painting a few years later. Ruth was not especially pleased by this intrusion into her new domain. Their daughter, Mary Lou (whose married name is Robinson), entered the field in 1977, inspired, of course, by her parents' success.

Ma and Pa Perkins work in oil; Mary Lou works in acrylics on canvas. The subject matter chosen by the two women is quite similar, centering on home, family, and church, and reflecting a life restricted by a traditional patriarchal society that relegated women to the kitchen, nursery, and church. Ruth Perkins shows an inventive use of perspective, often combining as many as four different viewpoints in a single painting. Both women have a knack for detail, bright colors, and fabriclike grounds. Ruth Perkins is perhaps the most creative of the lot. Her highly original composition and interesting juxtaposition of colors, as seen in such works as *Evening Entertainment,* offer something really new.

Ruth and Clarence Perkins reside in Transfer, Pennsylvania; Mary Lou Perkins Robinson lives in Warren, Ohio. The paintings of this remarkable trio have been shown at the John Judkyn Memorial at Freshford Manor, Bath, England, and at several galleries throughout the Midwest and the East.

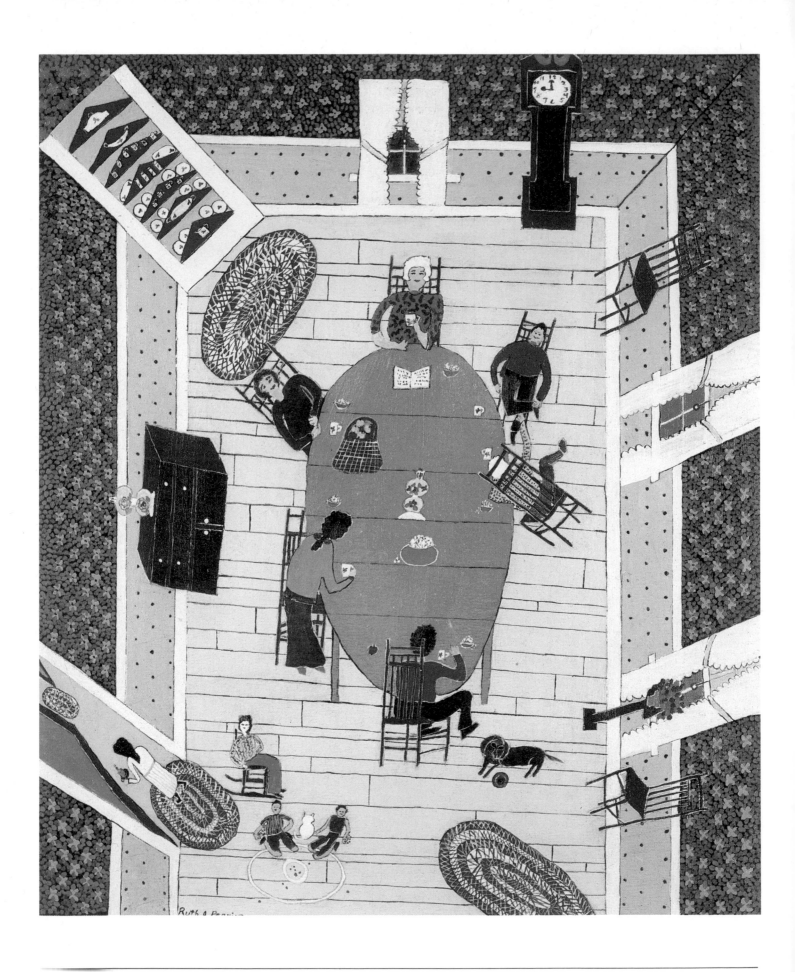

Mary Lou Perkins Robinson
*Lazy Sunday Afternoon*
1980
Acrylic on canvas; 24″ x 30″
Collection of the artist

*Opposite:* Ruth Perkins
*Evening Entertainment*
1979
Oil on canvas; 18″ x 24″
Private collection

Cy Perkins
*Side Show at the Circus*
1979
Acrylic on canvas; 18″ x 24″
Collection of the artist

# Joseph Pickett

It has been said that Joseph Pickett painted many pictures, but only a half-dozen works by this remarkable artist have survived. Pickett was born in 1848 in New Hope, Pennsylvania, where his father had come to work on the Lehigh Canal. Pickett lived in New Hope all his life, but he was somewhat of a wanderer, spending his springs and summers following the carnival circuit, running games of chance—chiefly shooting galleries. Every winter, Pickett would return to New Hope, and it was there that he settled down permanently following his marriage at the age of forty-five.

Pickett opened a small general store, and he began to paint in the store's back room. He had been trained as a carpenter and fancied himself something of a cabinetmaker. There is evidence that he had applied painted decoration to the booths he ran during his carnival period, but he appears to have done no serious painting until after his marriage. His working period extends roughly from the late 1890s until his death in 1918.

Pickett worked very slowly, spending years on a single painting. First using house paints, then oils on canvas, Pickett employed an impasto technique, putting down layer after layer of paint to create a surface so textured that it became almost a bas-relief. The feeling of solidity and depth was further enhanced by mixing sand, shell, and other materials into the pigment.

Like many folk artists, Pickett painted what he knew and painted it as he saw it. His subject matter was the area around New Hope, its history and topography. In *Washington Under the Council Tree*, he depicted the great oak under which General Washington supposedly planned the attack on Trenton. *Sunset, Lehigh Canal, New Hope* illustrates the area around the store in which he worked. His perspective reflected his preferences: important objects, such as the Council Tree, dominate the scene; items of lesser importance are made tiny despite their true size.

After his death, Pickett's work was neglected until it was discovered by a local artist in 1925. In 1930, several of Pickett's paintings appeared in the Newark Museum's first folk art exhibition, *American Primitives*. This was followed by inclusion in the Museum of Modern Art's *American Folk Art: The Art of the Common Man in America*, held in 1932. Paintings by Joseph Pickett are in the collection of the Newark Museum, Newark, New Jersey, among others.

Joseph Pickett
*Manchester Valley*
ca. 1914–18
Oil on canvas; 45½″ x 60⅝″
Museum of Modern Art, New York; gift of Abby Aldrich
Rockefeller

# Elijah Pierce

The folk carver Elijah Pierce was born near Baldwyn, Mississippi, in 1892. His
father, a former slave, was a church deacon, and Pierce was raised in an intensely
religious environment. Although the members of his family were field-workers,
Pierce did not like farming, and at the age of sixteen he began to work as a barber,
a trade he has followed ever since. Pierce became a preacher in 1920 and has also
pursued this calling.

Pierce began to carve in the 1920s, renewing a boyhood interest in the craft.
His first figure was an elephant made for his wife; since then he has produced
hundreds of animal figures. Pierce carves both religious and secular subjects. His
secular works are among his most inspired. His carved and painted reliefs are sometimes embellished with rhinestones and handfuls of glitter. Many of his works,
such as *Louis vs. Braddock* (a boxing scene) and a portrait of the legendary black
outlaw *Leroy Brown,* combine power with a sense of humor.

Pierce is best known for his religious carvings. These are based on biblical pas-

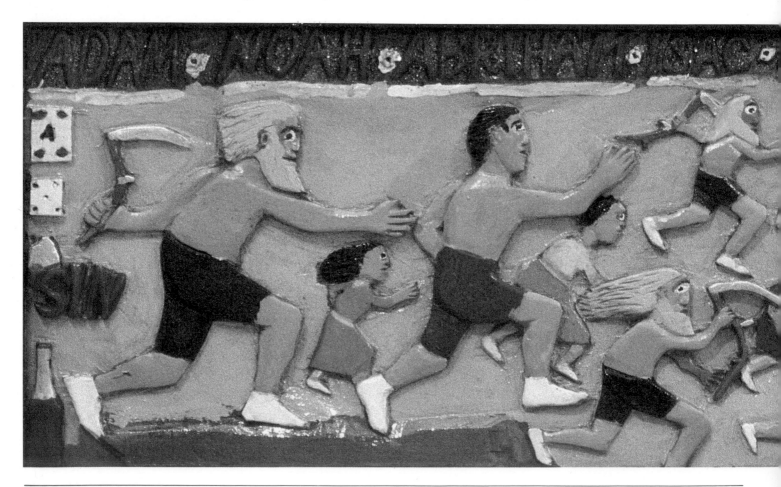

sages and depict well-known events, such as the story of Job, the Three Wise Men, and the making of the Ark. The evocative power of these works was well recognized by their creator, who often used them to illustrate his sermons, remarking that "Every piece of work I carve is a message, a sermon."

Pierce's two monumental achievements in this area are *The Book of Wood*, which consists of thirty-three separate scenes from the life of Christ; and *The Crucifixion*, a similar group of carvings that tells a story.

Although he saw his religious carvings as an aid to his preaching, Pierce recognized the possibilities of financial gain inherent in his secular works. As early as the 1930s, he began driving through the Ohio countryside selling his works at farms and fairs, and his barbershop in Columbus, Ohio, where he now lives, doubles as the Elijah Pierce Art Gallery. When business is slow, the proprietor carves, and the works are sold from the shop.

The works of Elijah Pierce have been widely exhibited. They were included in *Transmitters: The Isolate Artist in America* at the Philadelphia College of Art in 1981 and have been seen at the Pennsylvania Academy of Fine Arts, Philadelphia; the Krannert Art Museum, Champaign, Illinois; the Hopkins Hall Gallery, Columbus, Ohio; and the Phyllis Kind Gallery in New York City. Pierce's carvings are also in numerous collections.

Elijah Pierce
*Father Time Racing;* 1938
Carved and painted wood relief; 29" wide x 13" high
The Hall Collection of American Folk and Isolate Art

Elijah Pierce
*I Am the Door*
not dated
Carved and painted wood
relief; 13″ x 26″
Collection of Dr. Siri von
Reis

# Horace Pippin

One of the major folk painters of this century, Horace Pippin was born in West Chester, Pennsylvania, in 1888, the son of a poor laundress. His mother moved to Goshen, New York, where Pippin began, at the age of seven, to sketch in crayon and pencil. As soon as he was old enough, Pippin was put to work—as a clerk in a feed store, in a coal yard, as a hotel porter, and finally in a factory. In 1917, he joined the army and was sent to France, where he served on the Western Front until he was injured late in 1918. Returning to the United States with an arm partially paralyzed by a sniper's bullet, Pippin renewed his efforts to paint, gradually learning to use the injured member. He began with the creation of designs burned into wood with a hot poker (a technique known as pyrography) and later took up painting in oils on canvas, his preferred medium.

Beginning in 1929, Pippin created four related series of oils dealing with his World War I experiences, best known of which is the monumental *The End of the War: Starting Home.* Having purged himself of his war memories, he began to paint his childhood, his early years among the black communities of Goshen and West Chester. In some fifty to sixty genre paintings, portraits, and even still lifes, he captured the essence of the black experience in America as he saw it—its joys, hardships, nostalgia, and hope. It was during this period that one of his paintings, displayed in the window of a West Chester shoemaker's shop, was spotted by an art collector. It was 1937, and the discovery of John Kane and other folk painters had created a new interest in the genre. Pippin, too, was "discovered," and in 1938 four of his works appeared in the exhibition *Masters of Popular Painting,* at New York's Museum of Modern Art. Thereafter, Pippin's works were shown at important galleries, and he received the recognition his skills justified. He died in 1946.

For most of his career, Horace Pippin worked in a tiny, dark "second parlor" in his West Chester home, his canvas lighted only by a single unshaded bulb and his workday often stretching to seventeen hours. Where or how he worked mattered little—it was only important that he could work. As he once noted, "The pictures . . . come to me in my mind, and if to me it is a worthwhile picture, I paint it. I go over that picture in my mind several times, and when I am ready to paint it, I have all the details that I need. . . . My opinion of art is that a man should have love for it, because my idea is that he paints from his heart and mind."

*Page 242:* Horace Pippin
*The Love Note*
1944
Oil on canvas; 8″ x 10″
Collection of Richard and
Suzanne Barancik
Photo by David R. Williams

*Page 243:* Horace Pippin
*The Artist's Wife*
1936
Oil on canvas; 23¾″ x 16¾″
Collection of Richard and
Suzanne Barancik
Photo by David R. Williams

# Susan Powers

The still lifes of the young painter Susan Powers have been compared with the trompe l'oeil works of the well-known 19th-century American academic artist William Harnett. Like Harnett, Powers is fascinated with common, everyday objects —books, seashells, bottles, and teapots—and she renders them in a manner so lifelike that they "fool the eye" of the viewer, almost leading the viewer to believe that the objects themselves are present on the canvas.

The trompe l'oeil technique is uncommon with folk artists: some folk artists cannot produce a photographlike image, and those that can usually choose not to. Powers is fascinated with old objects (and cats), a carryover from long summers spent at her grandparents' Vermont farm, where she could roam through rooms filled with ancient books, bottles, and knickknacks. Assembling groups of these objects, she creates tightly woven compositions that are often colored in rich, dark hues appropriate to their age. These dark hues also reflect the shade and shadows of the somber rooms in which the objects would have been found.

Born in Glen Cove, New York, in 1954, Susan Powers now lives with her husband in New York City. She works in oils on canvas and delights in painting "objects that are rather ordinary on the surface but become a bit glamorous when one wonders about who made them, who used them, and how they came to be where they are now."

Paintings by Susan Powers are part of the permanent collection of the John Judkyn Memorial at Freshford Manor, Bath, England, and are in the collection of New York City's Chase Manhattan Bank. Her works have been shown at the Shirley Stuart Gallery in Southampton, New York, and the Jay Johnson America's Folk Heritage Gallery in New York City.

Susan Powers
*Calico Cat*
1983
Oil on canvas; 24" x 28"
Collection of Mr. and Mrs. Richard K. Simonson

Susan Powers
*Still Life with Seashells*
1982
Oil on canvas; 24″ x 30″
Collection of Mr. and Mrs. Robert Roskind

*Opposite:* Susan Powers
*Flowers in a Cricket Box*
1981
Oil on canvas; 14″ x 18″
Collection of Marcia Deschamps

Susan Powers

# Janis Price

It is rare that an artist achieves an important reputation in one field, let alone in two, but such is the case with Janis Price. Known for her bucolic oils on canvas, she has recently begun to create what she calls fabric art, complex pictures composed of sewn-together pieces of cut fabric. Although they are different in technique and materials, the two kinds of works produced by Price are very similar in feeling.

Born in Nashport, Ohio, in 1933, Janis Price developed an interest in art when she was very young. She later found that raising a family of three and working part-time left little opportunity for creative efforts. When her children were grown, she returned to her first love—art. She had no trouble deciding what to paint, for even as a child she had been fascinated by the tales told by her grandmother and great-grandmother of pioneer days in North Dakota and Oregon and had been a sharp observer of the Ohio countryside in which she grew up. Home life and the ways of the Ohio Amish have provided her with particularly fruitful inspiration, and many of her paintings illustrate 19th- and early 20th-century life as seen through the eyes of her grandparents.

Price's paintings may be less exacting in detail than the work of some of her contemporaries, but they have a patterned quality that is reminiscent of fabric. Varicolored houses seen against a background of fallen snow remind one of the well-known schoolhouse pattern quilts. It is no wonder that Price has taken to creating compositions similar to her paintings by cutting out small bits of cloth and sewing them together to create an interior or a landscape.

Janis Price lives and works in Newark, Ohio, usually putting in a seven-day week at her art. She has attracted nationwide attention but still remains the unassuming homebody who turned down a television appearance with Jimmy Dean in the belief that it was a joke. Her work is in the collection of the John Judkyn Memorial, Freshford Manor, Bath, England; and has been exhibited at London's Central School of Art & Design and the Piece Hall Gallery, Halifax, as well as various American galleries.

Janis Price
*Amish Clock Shop*
1980
Oil on canvas; 22″ x 30″
Collection of Alan and Risa
Nadel

Janis Price
*An Ohio Village*
1981
Oil on canvas; 24" x 36"
Collection of Francisco F. Sierra

Janis Price
*Brick Town*
1983
Oil on canvas; 36" x 48"
Collection of Mr. and Mrs. Michael Donovan

# Lamont ("Old Ironsides") Pry

The folk painter Lamont Pry takes as one of his main themes the circus, a reflection of the fact that he was involved with circuses and sideshows for most of his working life. Born in 1921 at Mauch Chunk, Pennsylvania, Pry left home at seventeen to join the Cole Brothers Flying Circus and became well known on the circuit for his hair-raising "Ladder in the Sky" act.

During World War II, Pry served as a crew member aboard a B-25 bomber and suffered serious injuries in a crash. His astonishing recovery from these near-fatal injuries earned him the nickname "Old Ironsides," which he continued to use after the war when he joined the Great Lucky Teeter Automobile Dare Devil Show. His career cut short by a heart condition, Ironsides Pry now resides in a nursing home.

Since his entry into the nursing home, Pry has begun to paint, working primarily in poster paint and pen on cardboard. His work, which reflects his own great spirit and enthusiasm for life, is an unusual mixture of scenes from his circus past, patriotic motifs, personal reminiscences, and current life. These paintings usually combine a series of individual vignettes with hand-written comments that explain the action and elaborate on the general theme. In *The Great Hoxie Brothers Circus*, bareback riders, a rhino in a cage, and an elephant act are set against a background of comments, such as "There's No Business Like Show Business," and personal messages, such as "God Bless You, Susan, My Darling."

Pry combines an unusual color sense and attention to detail with a personal iconography emphasizing surfaces decorated with series of dots and dashes, symbolic elements, such as the butterfly, and costumes of an almost tapestrylike nature. His work is in various collections and has been exhibited at the Abby Aldrich Rockefeller Folk Art Center, in Williamsburg, Virginia.

Lamont ("Old Ironsides") Pry
*The Great Hoxie Brothers*
*Circus*
not dated
Poster paint on cardboard; 21″ x 28″
Collection of Herbert W. Hemphill, Jr.
Photo by Bill Buckner

Lamont ("Old Ironsides") Pry
*Bathing Beauties*
1980
Poster paint on paper; 18″ x 30″
Collection of Lewis Allen

# Manuel Quiles

Manuel Quiles was born in 1908 in Puerto Rico and came to America at the age of sixteen. He settled in New York City and worked at various jobs until World War II. During the war, he learned woodworking as a mold maker, but he stopped working in wood after the war. Instead, he tried photography and then became a locksmith until his retirement. When he retired, he began carving whimsical figures for family and friends as a pastime. In 1908, with the encouragement of his family and an artist friend, he gathered a few of his works and went out to show them to the galleries in New York City. Within one day, he was well received and included in a group show, selling all of his work. This motivated him to carve full-time, and he has developed a unique style. His works have been exhibited at numerous galleries, including the Janet Fleisher Gallery in Philadelphia and the Thumbnail Sketch, in Oroville, California.

Manuel Quiles
*Rooster*
1980
Carved and painted wood;
19" high
Collection of Rubens Teles
Photo by Bill Buckner

Manuel Quiles
*Go-Go Dancer*
1980
Carved and painted wood
jewelry box; 29″ high
Private collection
Photo by Bill Buckner

# Martin Ramirez

Robert Bishop has called Martin Ramirez "the most significant 20th-century southwestern folk artist." Ramirez spent much of his life in the DeWitt State Hospital, a California institution for the insane. Born in Mexico around 1885, he came to the United States during his youth and appears to have worked at various menial tasks until well into his thirties. Sometime around 1915, he stopped talking, either because of some physical problem or because he simply no longer chose to speak. He continued to function in society until 1935, when he was diagnosed as a "paranoid-schizophrenic—deteriorated" and placed in a mental institution.

Little is known of his subsequent life other than the information that can be gleaned from hospital reports, but around 1945 Ramirez began to draw, employing combinations of pencil, crayon, and ink on paper. Between 1945 and his death in 1960, Ramirez created nearly two hundred drawings.

Ramirez is generally regarded as an isolate artist whose work stands outside the usual sources of American folk art, but it is evident that his drawings reflect his past and his culture. Subject matter, specifically the traditional religious motifs illustrated in works like *Our Lady of the Immaculate Conception*, reveals his awareness of the traditional Spanish-American *retablo* paintings of the Southwest. Design and composition often mirror the woven blankets and floor coverings (*jerga*) of the region.

Ramirez did not confine himself to religious art, however. He drew the cowboys of the West; strange, fantasy figures, such as the deity depicted in *Egyptian Scroll*; and even idealized street scenes. In all his works, Ramirez showed a remarkable sense of design, blending highly patterned grounds with abstracted images to produce drawings with the formal complexity of a Mondrian.

The drawings of Martin Ramirez have been exhibited at numerous galleries, including the Phyllis Kind Gallery, and they are also in various public and private collections.

Martin Ramirez
*Untitled*
not dated
Pencil, ink, and crayon on
paper; 17½″ x 31″
Collection of Herbert W.
Hemphill, Jr.
Photo by Bill Buckner

# E. "Popeye" Reed

The stonecarver E. "Popeye" Reed has lived his entire life in southern Ohio near the town of Jackson, where he was born. He began to carve at the age of fourteen, but it was many years before he turned from wood to the stone he now uses. For over twenty years he has worked in native stone, usually sandstone or limestone, employing whatever tools suit his purpose: a pocketknife, cold chisel, mallet.

Reed's sculpture always has a massive, earth-born quality, even though it is not always large. Some of his work, such as his well-known representations of Indians, are life-size, but many other pieces are much smaller. The subject matter varies greatly. Animals and birds are popular, but Reed also takes inspiration from such diverse sources as newspaper articles, Greek myths, magazine photographs, and postcards.

Reed lives and works in a one-hundred-fifty-year-old log house set in an isolated rural area, and he selects his stone from local quarries rather than employing imported materials. His figures are done both in the round and as bas-reliefs and possess a remarkable sensitivity despite the solidity of the materials from which they are shaped.

During the past decade Reed has appeared at various state and national fairs, exhibits, and cultural gatherings, exhibiting his sculpture and in some cases demonstrating his carving technique. He has worked at the Smithsonian Institution in Washington, D.C., as well as at the Ohio State Fair. His pieces are in various public and private collections.

E. "Popeye" Reed
*Angel*
not dated
Sandstone; 14¾" x 11½" x 4½"
Collection of Carolyn Oberst/Jeff Way
Photo by Keven Noble

E. "Popeye" Reed
*Eve*
1970
Carved sandstone; 14″ high
x 8½″ wide
Private collection
Photo by Bill Buckner

# Sandra Rice

Sandra Rice is one of the few contemporary folk artists working in clay. Born in Birmingham in 1949 and a graduate of the University of Alabama, she lives in Woodstock, Alabama. She began her work long after having married, established a family, and embarked on a successful professional career as a family counselor.

Her professional work seems to have influenced her art to a greater degree than with most folk sculptors. Dealing on a daily basis with people and their problems, joys, and interrelationships, she found herself drawn to the one medium—clay—that allowed her to best depict her characters in a lifelike situation. Her sculpted figures exist not in a vacuum but in an environment complete with furniture and smaller accessories, such as dishwares.

Rice's creations have personalities, another reflection of her experiences as a counselor. Women meeting for tea remove their joyful masks to reveal the sadness of their lives. A lonely man inspects the day's masks—which shall he wear? The figures have a disturbingly familiar look. Are they anyone we know?

The result perhaps of the demands of her professional life, Rice's artistic endeavors are highly structured. She usually works for two or three hours each day and for most of the weekends. Unlike most folk sculptors, she has the luxury of her own studio set in a secluded area near her rural home. She also has the enthusiastic support of her family, without which it would not have been possible to maintain such a schedule.

Rice feels that her efforts are not always successful. She tries to raise questions in the viewers of her figures—What are the little sculpted people thinking? How do they feel at the moment? What are their histories?—and she tries to give her pieces life that will concern the viewer. So difficult a goal is not always realized. Even so, the number of exhibitions in which Rice's work has appeared indicates that she draws a positive response. Among other places, her figures have been shown at the Perdue Gallery, the University of Alabama Gallery, and Anniston Museum of Natural History.

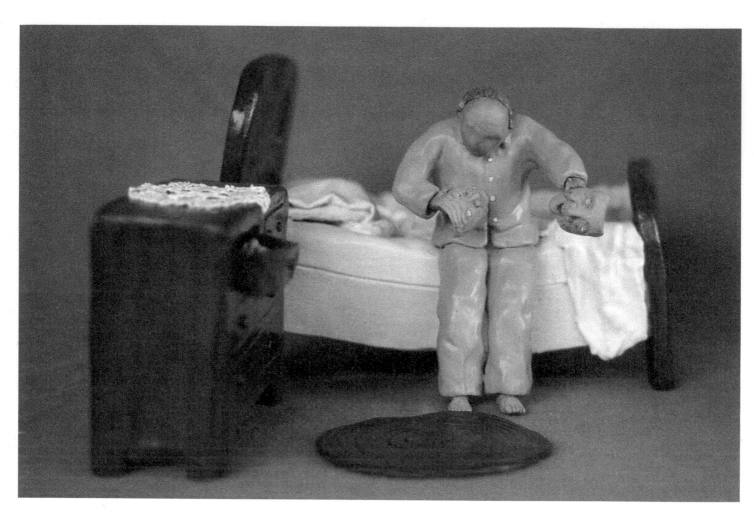

Sandra Rice
*Untitled*
1983
Baked clay and acrylic; fig-
ure, 7″ high; bed, 8½″ long
Collection of John Arnhold

Sandra Rice
*Old Friends*
1983
Baked clay and acrylic; figures, 17½″ high; sofa, 17½″
x 15″; brown chair, 13½″ x
10″; table, 13″ long, 6″ wide
x 6″ high
Collection of Dr. Howard
and Muriel Pottak

# Bill Roseman

Though he did not begin to paint steadily until his retirement from the New York public-school system in 1957, Bill Roseman comes naturally to the field. Born on Manhattan's Lower East Side in 1891, he grew up in a close family in which art and music were appreciated. He has two sons, both of whom have become noted artists. As a teacher, he concentrated on industrial arts and printing, and to further his own skills, he took courses for many years at the Brooklyn Museum's art school. However, Roseman is not an academic artist—his work is strictly in the folk vein, and he is fond of saying that the best thing his academic instructors did was to leave him alone when he was painting.

Roseman prefers to work in oils or acrylics on canvas, and his work reflects numerous inspirations. His strong religious background combined with his hatred of war can produce a powerful, almost demonic work such as *War Bird Threat to the World*. His almost lyrical studies memorialize his youth spent in the teeming streets of the Lower East Side, among the fishing wharves of Sheepshead Bay, and on the athletic fields of the metropolitan area. Roseman does not work entirely from memory, however. The older people with whom he dances, plays bingo, and talks at a local senior citizens' center also serve as inspiration for his work. Working alone in his kitchen, with a pet parakeet as his sole companion, Roseman paints, as he says, "At every opportunity." Most artists half his age would be glad to say the same.

Roseman's work is in many private collections, and his paintings have been exhibited at the Brooklyn Museum, the Metropolitan Museum of Art, and in such galleries as the International Art Exchange and AADA Artz Gallery, all in New York City.

Bill Roseman
*Untitled*
1964
Oil on canvas; 36″ x 31½″
Epstein/Powell American Primitives

Bill Roseman
*War Bird Threat to the World*
1960
Oil on canvas; 23″ x 24″
Collection of Dr. Robert Bishop
Photo by Bill Buckner

# Nellie Mae Rowe

It is often the fate of artists to be misunderstood, and such was the case with Nellie Mae Rowe. Though she could never remember not wanting to create, it was late in her life before she was able to do so without interference. As a child in Fayette County, Georgia, she made dolls by knotting the dirty laundry into appealing shapes, but her mother made her take them apart. As an adult, she began to fill the yard of her home in Vinings, Georgia, a suburb of Atlanta, with her creations, filling lawn furniture with her dolls and hanging ornaments of molded chewing gum inset with bits of glass and plastic from the trees. Neighbors responded by concluding she was a fortune teller and throwing rocks through her windows or destroying the dolls.

She retreated inside her ramshackle house and began to draw. Using colored pencils, crayons, and felt-tip pens, and working primarily on paper or cardboard, she created her own private cosmology. At first glance, her pictures seem aimless and cluttered, but upon closer observation they are seen to have a highly formalized structure. Sometimes compared to the work of the great painter Marc Chagall, Rowe's drawings are like jigsaw puzzles, with an overall symmetry in which every element is carefully related to and dovetailed into the total composition. While she lacked any formal training, Rowe had a highly formal sense of design—one which she could not, however, articulate, a common occurrence with folk artists. When asked how she thought out a picture, she responded, "I do as my mind tells me to do. Sometimes when I'm drawing I don't know what it's going to be, but I just keep on going."

Though devoutly religious, Rowe's work was little influenced by her faith. Her primary inspiration seemed to be childhood memories, with the shape and texture of the material on which she worked often influencing her approach. For example, cracks or lumps on a surface would often be translated into part of the overall composition.

Among others, the following public collections own pieces by Nellie Mae Rowe: High Museum of Art, Atlanta; National Museum of American Art, Washington, D.C.; Museum of International Folk Art, Santa Fe, New Mexico; and the Museum of American Folk Art in New York City. Her work has appeared in numerous individual and group shows, including the important *Missing Pieces: Georgia Folk Art, 1770–1976*, mounted in 1976 by the Georgia Council for the Arts and Humanities.

Nellie Mae Rowe
*The Fish*
not dated
Felt-tip pen on paper; 20″ x 24″
Collection of Lisa S. Roberts

Nellie Mae Rowe
*My House*
1979
Crayon on paper; 18″ x 24″
Epstein/Powell American
Primitives
Photo by D. James Dee

# Mark Sabin

Born in New York City in 1936 and raised in Florida, Mark Sabin began to paint seriously in 1972 after a varied career that included graduation from Columbia University Law School, several years in the U.S. Navy, and stints with entertainment firms, movie producers, and the theater. He had originally planned to be a lawyer, but he found himself gradually moving away from that field into others, including writing.

His first paintings—he works in acrylics on canvas—were produced as a diversion from the strain of composing the three as yet unpublished novels he has written. In time, the paintings became dominant, and Sabin found that he had become an artist.

Sometimes compared with the great French naive Rousseau, Sabin is a fantasy painter. His canvases, which have been described as "Freudian dreams, combining whimsical simplicity with sophisticated satire," blend elements in a juxtaposition that comes as a surprise to the viewer. In one of his paintings, a very modern-looking couple sit on a bench holding an infant whose carriage can be seen in the background. The infant is a leopard, a frequent symbol in Sabin's work. In another painting, *Fascination,* a group of men in tropical whites sit in the desert watching a television set. Above them, crouched on a branch and equally intent on the screen, is a leopard.

Sabin describes his work as "unconscious dictation" and disclaims any intent to satirize or to make political statements; nevertheless, there is a sophistication in his work that is lacking in most folk art.

Paintings by Mark Sabin are in various collections and have been exhibited at, among others, Atelier Lukacs in Montreal, Canada; Rolly-Michaux, Boston; the Portal Gallery in London; the Pratt Graphics Center and Hammer Galleries in New York City; and the Palm Beach Galleries in Palm Beach, Florida. His work has also appeared on magazine covers and record jackets.

Mark Sabin
*Lady on a Tiger*
1978
Acrylic on canvas; 24" x 32"
Collection of Mr. and Mrs. Robert Marcus

Mark Sabin
*Flying Wedding Couple*
1978
Acrylic on canvas; 14″ x 18″
Collection of Mr. and Mrs.
Richard Rosenthal

# Helen Salzberg

One of the most versatile of America's contemporary folk artists, Helen Salzberg was born in New York State in 1923 and now lives in Manhattan. She works in a wide range of materials, including acrylics, clay, and cut paper, and also constructs collages and makes prints.

Though her materials vary, most of her subject matter is derived from the Bible, chiefly from the Old Testament, which is a constant source of inspiration to her. Wedding feasts, street scenes, miraculous events, all are grist to her creative mill.

Salzberg's paintings are characterized by rich colors infused with the golden light of the Holy Land, and her subjects show the mixture of pride and humility that mark the true believer. Unlike most folk painters, she has been exposed to contemporary academic painting, and her work shows in some instances an awareness of academic technique, particularly that of the impressionist school.

Work by Helen Salzberg is in the permanent collections of Fordham University and the Central Synagogue, both in New York City, and is in private collections.

Helen Salzberg
*Wise Man*
1982
Reverse painting on glass;
9″ x 12″
Private collection
Photo by Bill Buckner

Helen Salzberg
*Wedding Ceremony*
1982
Reverse painting on glass;
11″ x 14″
Jay Johnson America's Folk
Heritage Gallery
Photo by Bill Buckner

# Jack Savitsky

Few folk artists have been propelled into the artistic limelight as quickly as was Jack Savitsky. Born in 1910 in the coal town of Silver Creek, Pennsylvania, he lived most of his life in another coal town, Lansford. He spent thirty-five years working in the coal mines and could hardly have hoped for any other future. Yet he had always loved to paint. At the age of ten, he had been given a box of watercolors and had done some sign painting and had even created murals for local barrooms. When he was sidelined, in 1959, by black lung and the shutting down of the local mines, he listened to his brother's suggestion that he paint. But he turned to painting more as a form of recreation than as an occupation.

As the number of his paintings grew, Savitsky and his wife began to sell them at local art shows, often for as little as one dollar each. His work attracted little interest until one of his paintings, *Train in Coal Town,* came to the attention of the well-known folk art collector Herbert W. Hemphill, Jr. Savitsky's career was launched. Since 1970, Savitsky has become a major figure in the folk art scene, and his works have become part of many collections and exhibitions.

Savitsky works on a variety of surfaces—canvas, Masonite, cardboard, wood, tin, and paper—and in several mediums—oils, watercolors, crayons, colored pencils, charcoal, and pen and ink. His studio is a cramped bedroom on the upper floor of his small two-family house overlooking the abandoned coal shafts of Lansford. His subject matter is the life that he knew in the mining town: the shafts; the coal trains; the haggard miners; the small, poor houses in which the miners lived. Although the subject matter is sometimes depressing, Savitsky's treatment of it never is. His bold colors and vibrant compositions transform the materials into highly decorative montages in which the two-dimensional perspective and the flat, linear design combine to create a unique surface.

The technique is entirely Savitsky's. As he says, "I'm self taught. . . . I paint from my imagination. If I can think of it, I can paint it."

Paintings by Savitsky are in various collections, including that of New York City's Museum of American Folk Art. In 1976, his work was included in a traveling bicentennial exhibition of folk art from the Herbert W. Hemphill, Jr., Collection for which a special catalog in Japanese was prepared.

Jack Savitsky
*Bootlegging Coal*
not dated
Oil on board; 26″ x 19½″
Collection of Lisa S. Roberts

Jack Savitsky
*Philadelphia and Reading Coal
and Iron Company*
1965
Colored pencil on paper;
21½″ x 15″
Private collection
Photo by Bill Buckner

# Antoinette Schwob

Unlike almost all other folk artists, Antoinette Schwob was not driven to her craft by a compulsion to paint. In fact, she took brush in hand only to quiet her artist husband who, having observed the way she arranged cookie-dough figures, became convinced she had the makings of a painter. To convince him that he was wrong, she painted her first picture. She was stunned at the result and plunged headlong into art.

Schwob's works, both landscapes and portraits, make an immediate impact through their almost desolate quality. Broad expanses of color are populated by tiny houses and figures. There is everywhere a sharp-edged quality and a clarity that make an instant impression. The viewer is thrust directly into a world populated by imaginary elements abstracted from Schwob's memories of a North Dakota childhood, dream images of turn-of-the-century France, and the insights into human personality acquired in forty-three years of work as a psychiatric nurse.

Schwob has worked steadily since 1950 and had her first one-woman show in 1968. She paints at home in New York City, employing an undeviating technique. First, a small pencil sketch is made, and from this the subject is roughed out on the canvas. However, as the painting takes shape, it seldom resembles the original sketch. During this process, no one is allowed to see the painting or even to discuss it. Like a chick from an egg, it just suddenly emerges.

Totally untrained, Schwob has achieved a style based on direct emotional impact rather than on detail. Even so, the details, which often reflect her memories of Cavalier, North Dakota, where she grew up, are astonishingly exact: an early Model T Ford could serve as a production-line prototype; houses appear as architectural drawings. Juxtaposed to these clear images are featherlike trees and an oddly distorted perspective. Nothing is ever predictable in Schwob's work.

Schwob's paintings are in the collections of the John Judkyn Memorial at Freshford Manor, Bath, England; the Museum of American Folk Art in New York City; and the Museum of International Folk Art in Santa Fe, New Mexico. *The Artist in His Studio* (a painting of her husband) appears in Robert Bishop's seminal work, *Folk Painters of America.*

Antoinette Schwob
*Cavalier High School*
1982
Oil on canvas; 30″ x 40″
Collection of Gary Daven-
port
Photo by Bill Buckner

Antoinette Schwob
*Mennonite Village*
1980
Oil on canvas; 36″ x 48″
Mr. and Mrs. Robert Marcus
Photo by Bill Buckner

*Following page:*
Antoinette Schwob
*Kathleen*
1982
Oil on canvas; 30″ x 40″
Private collection

# Mary Shelley

Mary Shelley is one of the few female carvers active today. Born in Doylestown, Pennsylvania, in 1950, she grew up on a farm and trained to be a writer. Her father was a commercial artist and part-time wood carver, and it was his gift of a carving of Mary as a child that inspired her own interest in the field. Since the early 1970s she has devoted herself to sculpture. She lives in West Danby, New York, in a house she built herself, and maintains a studio in nearby Ithaca, where she is also a professional sign painter.

Shelley carves aged pine boards using strong, deep strokes that create a three-dimensional effect. Her work, which is painted with acrylics, is based on sketches of incidents that she has witnessed or heard about. She describes her methods as follows:

> Drawing has always been the hardest part for me. I usually wait until I have a clear picture in my mind of what I can do. Then I set the drawing down as quickly as I can. Afterwards, I transfer it to my wood with carbon paper. My work is entirely carved, with no glued-on pieces. I use white pine or basswood, several boards fastened together by battens on the back. I paint the carving with acrylics, and afterwards varnish it.

Shelley's carvings are usually of rural scenes—farmers clearing a field or clean-up time at a small-town lunch room. The figures are strong and forceful, and animals often appear, especially dogs and cats, including the ones she keeps as pets. She prefers earth colors, and perspective is often "tilted up" to allow the viewer an unobstructed view of the entire scene.

In the past decade, Shelley has carved some one hundred fifty pieces, and her works have been seen at the Bede Gallery, Jarrow, England; the Arnot Museum, Elmira, New York; the National Museum of American Art, Washington, D.C.; and the Mid American Arts Alliance in Kansas City, Missouri. Examples are in the collection of the New York State Historical Association at Cooperstown.

Mary Shelley
*Floating Sauna Scene*
1983
Carved and painted wood
relief; 37″ x 35″
Private collection

Mary Shelley
*Bus Stop*
1982
Carved and painted wood
relief; 29″ x 30″
Collection of Myer and
Selma Mellman

Mary Shelley
*Clearing the Fields*
1983
Carved and painted wood;
42½″ x 32½″
Collection of Diane D. Kern

# Drossos P. Skyllas

Drossos P. Skyllas appears to have been one of the very few 20th-century folk artists who thought of themselves as artists throughout their lives. Born in Kalymnos, Greece, in 1912, Skyllas worked for his father's tobacco business until just after World War II, when he came to the United States and eventually settled in Chicago.

His father had not allowed Skyllas to paint while he was in Greece, but he began to do so as soon as he arrived in Chicago. Except for the influence of Greek icons, which he could have acquired as easily in Greece as in his many trips to the Art Institute of Chicago, he shows little sign of academic tendencies. But he was a remarkably capable technician. Moreover, he thought of himself as an artist and actively sought commissions to paint portraits—at prices ranging up to $30,000, a very high fee for even an academic and recognized portraitist. Not too surprisingly, no one seems to have purchased his services. His wife, Iola, supported them both while he devoted himself full-time to his painting. From the late 1940s until his death in 1973, Skyllas produced some thirty-five paintings.

Skyllas worked in oil on canvas, creating remarkable compositions that focus on religious figures from the Greek Orthodox pantheon and on surreal landscapes, the vaguely Oriental elements of which are less striking than the jewellike detail he achieved. Despite his visits to the Art Institute and his seeking of patrons in the art world, Skyllas was an isolated painter whose work is almost totally removed from both the mainstream of American academic art and most folk art. Rich with symbolism, his compositions convey a secret message to the initiated—of which, alas, there were few.

Drossos P. Skyllas's paintings are in various public and private collections and have been exhibited at the Philadelphia College of Art.

Drossos P. Skyllas
*The Greek Bishop*
ca. 1965
Oil on canvas; 63″ x 40½″
Collection of Richard and
Suzanne Barancik
Photo by David R. Williams

*Opposite:* Drossos P. Skyllas
*Red Head*
undated
Oil on canvas; 54″ high x
40″ wide
The Hall Collection of
American Folk and Isolate
Art

Drossos P. Skyllas
*The Blue Kiosk*
1953
Oil on canvas; 20″ x 31½″
Collection of Richard and
Suzanne Barancik
Photo by
David R. Williams

# Susan Slyman

Though superficially similar, the work of Susan Slyman differs greatly from that of most of the artists discussed in this book. Born to a middle-class family in Washington, D.C., and a graduate of a prestigious eastern girls' school, she was exposed at an early age to academic painting and took art courses in college. As a result, her work has a sophisticated look that is not unlike that of contemporary advertising art. Her compositions are organized with a sophisticated eye and feature broad expanses of carpet or meadow across which dancers or horses (one of her artistic obsessions and the subject of most of her early work) flow in stylized waves of motion. Line and color are skillfully manipulated to obtain maximum effect, and details are calculated to enhance the overall purpose of the composition rather than being spontaneous expressions of the artist's past, as is the case with true memory painters.

Rather than relying on memory, Slyman draws her inspiration from stories she has read, things she sees, or tales of olden times related by country people in the vicinity of the small town where she now resides. Animals and music are her great loves, and the former figure prominently in many of her works while the latter is reflected in the lyrical quality of her design. She feels that her own distinction between past and present is at times somewhat hazy, and although most of her paintings are set at the turn of the century, the events depicted may be ones that occurred recently. They are simply transferred to an earlier temporal setting.

Susan Slyman lives in Mt. Kisco, New York, where she works in an attic studio putting in six to seven hours each day at her craft. Her works have been shown at the Danbury, Connecticut, Arts and Crafts Fair; at the Armonk, New York, art show; and at the Bridge Gallery in White Plains, New York.

Susan Slyman
*Shaking the Cat*
1982
Acrylic on canvas; 16″ x 20″
Collection of Mr. and Mrs.
Michael M. Minchin, Jr.

Susan Slyman
*Hunter Trial*
1981
Acrylic on canvas; 14″ x 18″
Collection of Mr. and Mrs.
George Newall

Susan Slyman
*Waltz in the Grand Ballroom*
1982
Acrylic on canvas; 18″ x 24″
Collection of Mr. and Mrs.
Bernard Morse

# Helen Fabri Smagorinsky

The seldom accurate but often repeated story of the folk artist as social recluse is no more clearly refuted than in the life of the artist Helen Fabri Smagorinsky. Born in Rochester, New York, in 1933, she has lived much of her life in the nearby town of Brockport surrounded by a family that provides much of the inspiration for her work. Her dining room is her studio, her children are both her models and her critics. The result is a soft bucolic art that glows with the colors of country summers and autumns and is alive with activities, such as the Fourth of July parade, that still take place in upstate New York.

Though lacking both formal training and a family tradition in the arts, Smagorinsky painted still lifes as a young girl, and once her children were old enough to allow her the time, she began again to experiment with colors. Always interested in the effect of paint on aged wood, she first composed landscapes on old boxes. For a long time these were all winter scenes; Smagorinsky notes that it took her some time to learn how to mix the greens required for grass and leaves. Once this was mastered, however, she portrayed the scenery of her area at all seasons, sometimes combining two periods of the year in the same work.

Smagorinsky's present work consists primarily of oils on canvas, though she still sometimes uses wood, finding that the grain enhances the affect she seeks to achieve. Subject matter may be contemporary, but it is more often historical in nature, depicting the Brockport area and the old Erie Canal, on whose banks the town sits, as they appeared in the late 19th century. An avid local history buff, the artist is well aware of major events that have occurred in the area, and the buildings and locales she paints are usually ones that stand or have stood in Genesee County, an area rich in Victorian architecture.

An artist whose work is just beginning to attract critical attention, Helen Fabri Smagorinsky's work has been shown at the Genesee County (New York) Museum and at local galleries in her area. Appropriately enough in light of her close attachment to home and family, one of her paintings now graces the cover of a cookbook!

Helen Fabri Smagorinsky
*Parade on Main Street*
1982
Oil on canvas; 24" x 36"
Collection of Philip Bernet

Helen Fabri Smagorinsky
*Genesee County*
1981
Oil on canvas; 16″ x 20″
Collection of Robert and
Miriam Karlin
Photo by Bill Buckner

# Fannie Lou Spelce

The personal deprivations, discrimination, and sense of loss that have fueled the work of so many folk artists are singularly lacking in the paintings of Fannie Lou Spelce. In fact, her life and the work in which it is reflected resemble the small-town dream to which many Americans aspire.

Born in the hill community of Dyer, Arkansas, in 1908, Spelce grew up in a simple but moderately prosperous family and pursued a successful career as a nurse. She appears to have had little interest in art until she was in her fifties, at which time she enrolled in a painting course because she was bored with her long summer vacations from a job as a school nurse.

The course instructor took one look at Spelce's first effort and declared her a "primitive." He told her to leave the class and paint on her own. She took his advice and has since produced over two hundred oils on canvas. Most of her paintings depict rural southwestern life as she recalls it: a bucolic pattern of barn raisings, harvest festivals, quilting bees, dances, and family gatherings. Nothing unpleasant ever intrudes upon these brightly colored canvases with their tapestry-like backgrounds and decorative details. As Spelce has remarked, "I don't like to remember ugly things, only happy things." Spelce's selective memory may well be partly responsible for the enthusiasm with which many Americans have embraced her paintings.

Spelce's paintings combine busy backgrounds with foregrounds devoted to minute detail—needles in small hands or words on tiny newspapers. In some cases, several scenes are integrated, collagelike, into a single canvas.

The paintings of Fannie Lou Spelce are widely collected and have been shown throughout the United States. Her works have been exhibited at the Museum of American Folk Art in New York City; the Dallas Museum of Fine Arts; the White Museum in San Antonio, Texas; and the Laguna Gloria Art Museum in Austin, Texas. Her work has also been featured in a variety of publications, including the *New York Times*, *Smithsonian* magazine, and the *Wall Street Journal*. She now lives and works in West Lake Hills, near Austin.

Fannie Lou Spelce
*Peach Season*
1968
Oil on canvas; 24″ x 30″
Spelce Family Collection

Fannie Lou Spelce
*Quilting Bee*
1966
Oil on canvas; 28″ x 38″
Spelce Family Collection

# Mose Tolliver

Artists are sometimes born of adversity, and such was the case with Mose Tolliver. The child of a farm family, he was one of twelve children born to a farmer working land near Montgomery, Alabama. He left school after the second grade to go to work and learned the upholstery trade and how to make furniture. In the early 1970s, while working for a furniture store, his foot was crushed in an accident. Unable to work, he began to paint to occupy his time.

Tolliver's paintings are among the most unusual produced by the school of black folk artists. The majority are representations of people or animals, but he also paints landscapes. Colors are applied in thick masses within the most elementary of compositional frameworks to create what Robert Bishop has called "quasi-representational figures, hauntingly abstracted."

The materials used are wall or exterior house paints (what Tolliver refers to as "pure paint," as opposed to artists' colors) on cardboard, wood, paper, or book covers. Tolliver has even worked on the back of an upholstered chair, and it is clear that to him the medium is not the message. His paintings are often inspired by illustrations in children's books, but they are never mere copies and are done with great care, right down to the hanger with which each is equipped. The hanger is especially important, as Tolliver needs to hang a picture and to look at it for a while before he is sure that it is properly finished.

As with some other fantasists and memory painters, Tolliver works compulsively, often late into the evening. He sometimes springs up in the middle of the night when an idea for a painting strikes him. His work, which at its best has the power and drama of certain Picasso examples, is in various collections and has been exhibited at the Philadelphia College of Art; the National Museum of American Art, Washington, D.C.; and the Brooklyn Museum, New York.

Mose Tolliver
*Telma*
1973
House paint on wood;
15″ x 20″
Private collection

Mose Tolliver
*The Morning After;* 1976
House paint on wood; 17″ x 20″; private collection

# Edgar Tolson

The religious orientation of the sculpture produced by Edgar Tolson belies his own rather remarkable background. Born in Lee County, Kentucky, in 1904, and now a resident of the town of Compton in the same state, Tolson has worked at a variety of jobs—including those of farmer, cobbler, and chairmaker—and has served as an itinerant preacher who boasts of blowing up his own church and of setting fire to two of his own homes. For some thirty-five years, Tolson has been a wood carver, although he occasionally works in stone.

Tolson's work comes out of his background. He has lived his life in the Appalachian Mountains and can recall the details of blood feuds, strikes in the mines, and domestic violence. Although he is a preacher, he has done his share of whiskey drinking and tobacco chewing, dancing and fiddling. His major works, such as the series on the Expulsion from Paradise and the story of Cain and Abel, say less about the traditional biblical themes than they do about the life of man in general. The carved and painted wooden figures with their stony-faced frontality have the feel of Gothic images, but they also reflect the isolated life of the hill people of Appalachia, who have learned to conceal their feelings—even from themselves.

Certain elements of Tolson's work, particularly the handling of animals and trees, reflect the whittling tradition that has existed in the mountains for generations (Tolson's own family settled in this country in the 17th century); but the power and directness of his totemic figures finds little kinship other than with the often touching gravestone carvings that can be found in the old cemeteries of the Atlantic coast.

Tolson has little to say about his work. His theory of creation is a simple one: "You don't make it with your hands. You form it with your hands. You make it with your mind." True to this precept, Tolson continues to work.

The sculpture of Edgar Tolson is in various museum collections, including that of the Museum of American Folk Art. It formed an important part of the exhibition *Folk Sculpture USA*, mounted in 1976 by the Brooklyn Museum.

Edgar Tolson
*The Barring of the Gates of Paradise*
1969
Carved and assembled wood, partially painted; 15″ x 19¾″
The Hall Collection of American
Folk and Isolate Art

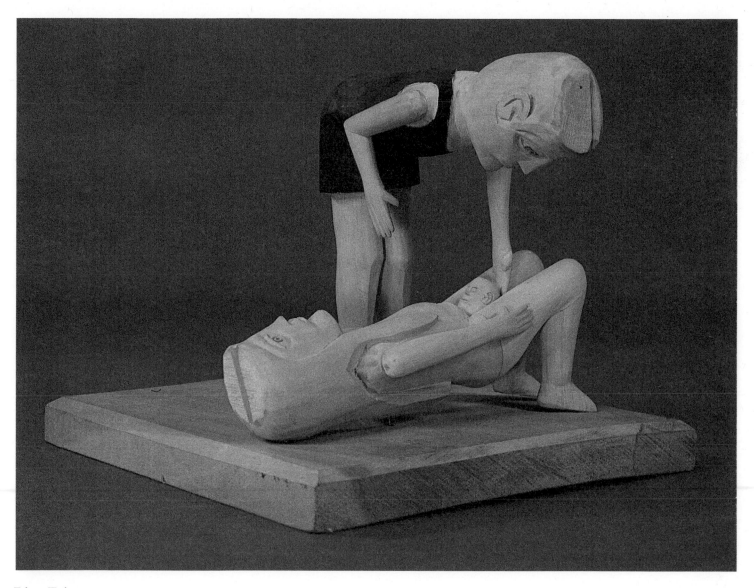

Edgar Tolson
*Birth of Cain*
not dated
Carved and assembled wood;
8″ x 9½″
The Hall Collection of
American Folk and Isolate
Art

Edgar Tolson
*Paradise*
not dated
Carved and assembled wood;
12″ x 17½″
The Hall Collection of
American Folk and Isolate
Art

# Bill Traylor

Born a slave on the plantation of George Traylor in 1854, the folk artist Bill Traylor (like many slaves, he took the name of the owner of the plantation where he was born) lived most of his life near Benton, Alabama, working as a field hand at the same farm where he grew up. In 1938, Traylor moved to nearby Montgomery, where he tried working in a shoe factory. Crippled by rheumatism, Traylor soon found himself an unemployed recipient of government welfare payments. With his days reduced to idleness, Traylor began—at the age of eighty-five—to draw. Turning to art appears not to have been a conscious decision: as the artist once said, "It just come to me."

At first he worked with whatever materials were available, pen or pencil and scrap paper or cardboard. As his confidence increased, he employed crayons, watercolors, and gouache. The works he created have often been compared to the ancient cave paintings of Lascaux in France and Altamira in Spain. They are stark, ideographic representations of men, animals, and objects—tools, furniture, or household implements—united in compositions that frequently appear to have little internal cohesiveness. In the more complex works, a scene appears at the left and runs off the right—a fragment of action without beginning or end.

The figures in these drawings are often strange or violent. A man without legs rolls across the page on a rockerlike platform. Drunkards dance with their bottles or are struck down by fellow tipplers. Traylor's creations appear to reflect his life— the drawings are visual reminiscences of events he either saw or was involved in.

From 1939 to 1942, Traylor worked in Montgomery in an almost compulsive way, turning out sketches from dawn till dusk. During World War II, Traylor moved north to be with relatives. If he worked during that period, no traces of his art have been found. In 1946, Traylor reappeared in Montgomery and began to draw again with the same frantic need. This time his career was brief; he died the following year.

The works of Bill Traylor have been exhibited at, among other places, the R. H. Oosterom Gallery, New York City; the New South Art Center in Montgomery, Alabama; and as part of the show *Southern Works on Paper, 1900–1950*, circulated in 1981–1982 by the Southern Arts Federation.

Bill Traylor
*Man, Dog, and Bird*
not dated
Watercolor on paper; 12″ x 12″
Collection of Mr. and
Mrs. Maurice C. Thompson, Jr.

William Traylor
*Pig*
not dated
Watercolor on cardboard;
12″ x 12″
Collection of Mr. and Mrs.
Maurice C. Thompson, Jr.

Bill Traylor
*Woman*
not dated
Watercolor on paper;
17½″ x 11⅜″
Collection of Dorothy
and Leo Rabkin
Photo by Bill Buckner

# Inez Nathaniel Walker

The black artist Inez Nathaniel Walker began to draw while in prison. Incarcerated from 1971 to 1974 at the Bedford Hills Correctional Facility in New York State, she sought art as a refuge from the daily horrors of prison existence. As she once remarked, referring to that period, "There were all those bad girls talking dirty all the time, so I just sit down at a table and draw." Ironically, much of Walker's early work focused on the very people whose influence she sought to escape, those "bad girls." When she was released in 1974, she returned to life as a migrant worker. Walker's drawings, typically done in pencil, ink, crayon, or a combination of these on paper, began to encompass a larger and more diverse cast of characters after her release. By this time she had also attracted a following, and like many folk artists her work was influenced by the needs and demands of her collectors.

Walker remains very much her own person. Her work, though superficially childlike, has a highly structured quality that blends the stylized rigidity of 19th-century folk portraits with the coloring and patterned surfaces of a Matisse. There is a textile quality to most of her backgrounds, and it is often carried over into the clothing, hair, and even the features of her subjects. Portraiture remains Walker's strong suit. Not exact portraiture, though; she does not work from life. She has explained, "I can't look at nobody and draw. Now that's one thing I wished I could do. But I can't. I just draw by my own mission, you know. I just sit down and start to draw."

The drawings of Inez Walker are in various public and private collections, including that of the Museum of American Folk Art, New York City.

Inez Nathaniel Walker
*Double Portrait*
1976
Pencil and felt-tip pen on
paper; 17½″ x 23½″
Collection of Rubens Teles
Photo by Bill Buckner

# George White

In a self-composed "certificate of award" prepared the year before he died, George White described himself as a maker of "leathercraft, wood carver, sculpture, artist, cabinetmaker, mounting, brick mason, plumber, electrician, physiologist, farming, interior decorator, train horses and dogs, building contractor, and barber." He was even more. Born in Cedar Creek, Texas, of mixed black, Mexican, and American Indian ancestry, White lived a life symbolic of the "macho" West. At various times he worked as a farmer, cowpoke, deputy sheriff, rodeo rider, oil-field worker, and soldier.

When he began his artistic career, in 1961, at the age of fifty-eight, he incorporated much of this past experience into his work. Rodeos, battles between cowboys and Indians, ranch scenes, boxing matches, lumber camps, and hunting trips were depicted. The media in which these scenes appeared were varied and complex. Many of the traditional western views were carved in relief, usually on pine, and then painted in oils. However, the forty-odd pieces White left also include ingenious mixed-media constructions in which carving is combined with elements of collage—paper, leather, fabric, and metal—that were grafted to the surface to provide an exciting three-dimensional story. Also present in his collection were sculptural carvings, some of which were animated. Most of the latter were assemblages, grouping several figures in an action-filled diorama.

While many of White's creations focused on the outdoor life of the old West, others reflected his awareness of the role of blacks in the building of that area—the hardships, poverty, and discrimination that were daily facts of minority existence. Thus, *The Land of Cotton* combines in collage a snatch of text extolling the invention of the cotton gin with a relief carving of blacks toiling in the cotton fields beneath the watchful eyes of the white overseer.

Works by George White have been widely exhibited in the Southwest, where they have been seen at, among others, the Waco Creative Art Center, Waco, Texas; the San Antonio Museum of Art; and the Delahunty Gallery in Dallas.

George White
*The Land of Cotton*
1967
Oil on wood; 20″ x 24″
Collection of Dr. Siri von
Reis
Photo by Bill Buckner

# Philo Levi ("Chief") Willey

One of the 20th century's prolific folk painters, Philo Levi Willey has produced some three hundred ninety-six watercolor and pencil drawings and over four hundred acrylics, a medium he turned to after his reputation was well established. Born in Canaan, Connecticut, in 1887, Willey had the sort of life folk painters are made from. At the age of twelve, with a five-dollar bill in his pocket, he left home. During the next thirty years or so he wandered about the United States, soaking up experience and working at a remarkable variety of jobs, including farmer, lumberman, storekeeper, fireman, deckhand on a steamboat, wagon driver for the Barnum & Bailey circus, and even cowpoke on the ranch in Wyoming owned by Buffalo Bill Cody's family.

In 1932, he settled in New Orleans. He went to work for the local sewage-and-water board, eventually rising to become its chief police officer—hence the nickname "Chief," which has stuck with him ever since.

The Chief retired from the force in 1966, and, four years later, casting about for something to occupy his time, he started to paint. He was an instant success. As he tells it:

> I went down to Jackson Square with the first three pictures that I had, and as I got the last one hung up on the fence, a lady came up and slapped me on the back and she says, "I want those pictures, and I'll give you seven and a half apiece for them."

The Chief never looked back. He started turning out works, first in watercolor and pencil, later in acrylics, and his art was received with tremendous enthusiasm by collectors. Though much of what he does reflects his varied background, the Chief is more a fantasist than a memory painter. His works are often peopled with an iconography of recurrent figures, including Preacher Bear, a palomino horse, a bowlegged turtle, and a man in bright-red pants. The paintings also have a charming, layered effect: a bright-blue sky filled with puffy white clouds above and bands of houses, fields, and creatures alternating below. Perhaps most important, his works convey a sense of peace and organization that is most attractive in our sometimes chaotic world.

Paintings by Chief Willey are in the collections of the Museum of International Folk Art, Santa Fe, New Mexico; the New York State Historical Society at Cooperstown, New York; and many private collections.

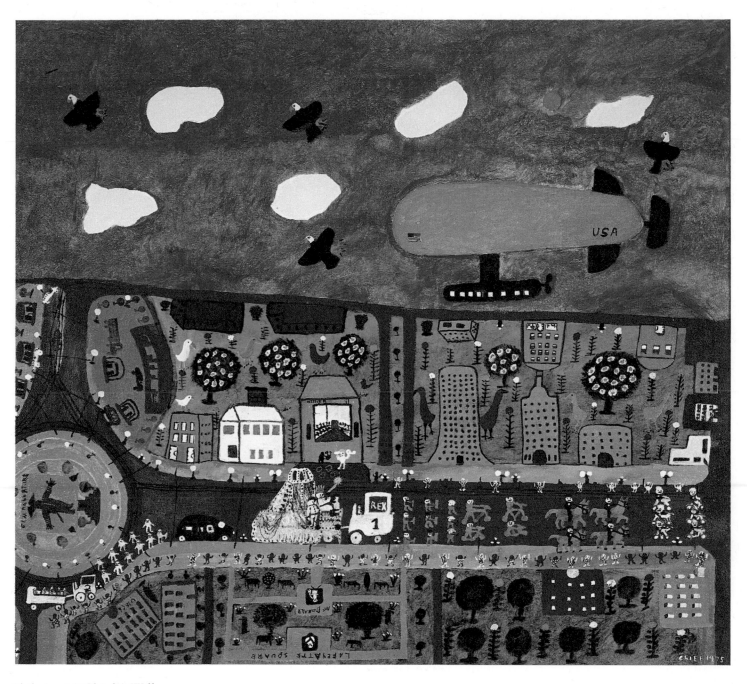

Philo Levi ("Chief") Willey
*Mardi Gras*
1975
Oil on canvas; 36″ x 40″
Private collection

Philo Levi ("Chief") Willey
*Gospel Bear*
1977
Oil on canvas; 16″ x 20″
Private collection

# Luster Willis

Few folk artists excel in both painting and sculpture, but such is the case with Luster Willis. Born near Terry, Mississippi, in 1913, Willis is now retired, but he has worked as a farm laborer, barber, and woodcutter and served in the U.S. Army during World War II. Even as a child, Willis loved to draw, and he recalls being reprimanded by schoolteachers for sketching during classes.

Willis's paintings display more complexity than his carvings. He usually works in watercolors on paper or poster board, sometimes varying the texture with finger paint or even shoe polish. The materials he works with are ordinary—what he does with them sets him apart from other folk artists. He is a far more skilled draftsman than most folk artists, and he produces work embodying complex narratives that employ symbolic statements to illustrate social commentary. For example, in the painting *Rich Man/Poor Man*, a thin man with a dry bone confronts a fat man holding a cigar. The complexity of the subject matter is matched by complexity of construction. Willis often works within several levels, achieving a feeling of depth through the collagelike application of paper cuttings. In some works he cuts away the body of the piece to create a silhouette; others are highlighted by the application of gold or silver glitter.

The subject matter of Willis's paintings is both secular and religious. Among the secular works are family portraits and scenes of traditional community activities, such as dances, parties, and weddings. His religious works include biblical tales and the depiction of church services.

Compared to his paintings, Willis's carvings are quite simple and direct. He carves canes—always popular with southern black carvers—that terminate in fully carved figures or in busts. These pieces display a vague resemblance to certain African fetish figures, but there is no indication that Willis is either familiar with or inspired by those works.

Works by Willis are in various collections, including those of the Center for Southern Folklore at Memphis, Tennessee, and the Center for the Study of Southern Culture at Oxford, Mississippi. Examples of his work were included in the exhibition *Made by Hand: Mississippi Folk Art*, mounted by the Mississippi State Historical Museum, Jackson.

Luster Willis
*Night Ladies*
1981
Poster paint on paper;
14" x 20"
Epstein/Powell American
Primitives

# Joseph E. Yoakum

The folk painter Joseph E. Yoakum was born in 1886 on the Navajo reservation at Window Rock, Arizona. He is believed to have been an Indian, but he sometimes referred to himself as "an old black man." Yoakum's childhood was spent on a farm near Walnut Grove, Missouri. Farm life appears to have had little appeal for him, for in his early teens he ran away to join the circus.

He worked as a roustabout, handyman, and valet for several traveling circuses during the early 1900s, including those of Buffalo Bill and the Ringling Brothers. Sometime later, he became a world traveler, working on—and sometimes stowing away aboard—a variety of ships. Yoakum served in the U.S. Army during World War I and later married and fathered five children. His whereabouts from the early 1920s until the 1960s are uncertain: he appears to have traveled widely, to have worked at many jobs, and to have married for a second time.

In 1962, he settled in Chicago and remained there until his death in 1972. Yoakum was famous for telling stories about his life. Some people have questioned his tales—Could one man really have seen so much?—but no one questions his genius. Drawing on both his store of experience and his imagination, Yoakum turned out a substantial number of drawings, most of them watercolors or pastels on paper, though some early examples were in pen or pencil with little color.

Almost all of his pieces were landscapes, and they were created by a process Yoakum called "spiritual unfoldment," by which he seems to have meant that his works were blends of fact and fancy revealed to him as he worked rather than planned in advance. The results were beautifully drafted views of field, forest, and hill, featuring an emphatic line and a strong chromatic sense. Especially during the last years of his life, these drawings were produced with great rapidity—one or two each day.

Drawings by Joseph E. Yoakum have been exhibited at the School of the Art Institute of Chicago; the Pennsylvania State University Art Museum, University Park, Pennsylvania; the Whitney Museum of American Art, New York City; and the University of Rhode Island in Kingston. He was featured in the show *Transmitters: The Isolate Artist in America,* at the Philadelphia College of Art in 1981.

The Scrol above town of Ein Gedi
west of Dead Sea by Essenes
above town of Ein Gedi
by Joseph. E. Yoakum

Joseph E. Yoakum
*The Scrol Above Town of Ein Gedi West of Dead Sea by Essenes*
1968
Watercolor and ink on paper; 12″ x 19″
Collection of Dr. Siri von Reis
Photo by Bill Buckner

Joseph E. Yoakum
*Mt. Polkin Near Strelka Peak,*
*Central Siberian Uplands of*
*Soviet Russia*
1966
Watercolor and pen on
paper; 12″ x 19″
Collection of Dr. Siri von
Reis
Photo by Bill Buckner

# Malcah Zeldis

One of the most widely exhibited contemporary folk painters, Malcah Zeldis combines an almost volcanic use of pure color with a seething imagery that draws on not only her own experiences but also on current social and political issues and her strong Jewish background.

Born in New York City in 1931, Zeldis moved at an early age to Detroit, where she was raised in near poverty. Although she always wanted to paint, she did not begin work for many years. In the interim, she worked on collective farms in Israel, where she went at the age of eighteen, married, and raised two children. In 1958, she returned to New York, and as her children grew she found her thoughts turning more and more to art. By the late 1960s she was fully immersed in her painting, an experience she has described in her own words:

> It is only recently, now that my children are grown, that I have been able to return to painting as though I were a traveler returning to my native shore. Suddenly, all the years of waiting have been erased and the emotional depths from which my paintings arise give me a great sense of fulfillment. . . . All my life seems to have taken on a mystery and beauty for which I am deeply grateful.

Zeldis's paintings have a power and an immediacy with which some people may be uncomfortable. Not only are the colors raw and vibrant, but the subject matter, particularly the scenes based on Old Testament subjects, is not always readily accessible. Her paintings of New York City, however, such as *Street Scene* and *Times Square,* boil with the life and excitement of the big city, and her moving depictions of the trials of the Russian dissident Solzhenitsyn touch a universal human heartstring.

Malcah Zeldis works in oils on Masonite. Her paintings are part of the permanent collections of the Musée d'Art Naïf de l'Ile de France, Paris; the Museum of American Folk Art, New York City; the Museum of International Folk Art, Santa Fe, New Mexico; and the Kresge Art Center Gallery, East Lansing, Michigan. They have been exhibited throughout this country and in Europe and have been illustrated in twenty books and publications on folk art.

330

*Opposite:* Malcah Zeldis
*Black Cat*
1980
Oil on Masonite; 14″ x 16½″
Collection of Rubens Teles
Photo by Bill Buckner

Malcah Zeldis
*Lincoln Near Tent*
1975
Oil on Masonite; 24″ x 32″
Collection of Dr. Robert
Bishop

Malcah Zeldis
*Solzhenitsyn After Solitary Confinement*
1976
Oil on Masonite; 32″ x 32″
Collection of Mr. and Mrs. Maurice C. Thompson, Jr.

# Larry Zingale

Born in the rural New York State community of Florida, Larry Zingale has been interested in art since he was a child. He first turned his hand to landscapes, but during the past decade he has come to focus on what he now sees as his major area: the painting of portraits.

Zingale's portraits are characterized by strong colors, a relatively uncomplex composition, and great attention to facial expressions. Whether the subject is a dog or a notorious outlaw, the artist shows great concern for expressing character through the delineation of facial features. He works from life or from photographs —he based a series of portraits on police-department mugshots of wanted criminals. One of the most successful of Zingale's works is a three-quarter-length frontal view of Bruno Hauptmann, the man executed for the kidnapping and murder of the Lindbergh baby.

A sports fan, Zingale also portrays baseball players, including Babe Ruth, and has even done a self-portrait in which he appears wearing the uniform of the old Brooklyn Dodgers. He also does paintings of sports events, such as baseball games.

Zingale works in oils on canvas at his studio in New York City. Painting slowly and carefully, he rarely completes more than one dozen paintings in a year. Small though this output may seem, it has attracted nationwide attention. His works are in the collection of the Museum of International Folk Art, Santa Fe, New Mexico, and have been exhibited at the Museum of American Folk Art in New York City; the Stamford, Connecticut, Museum; the Nassau County Fine Arts Museum, Roslyn, New York; and the Wilson Arts Center in Topeka, Kansas. His paintings are owned by major individual and corporate collections, including that of the Chase Manhattan Bank.

Larry Zingale
*Mug Shot of Judy Garrity*
1980
Oil on canvas; 22″ x 28″
Collection of Richard and
Lois Rosenthal

Larry Zingale
*Bruno Hauptmann*
1981
Oil on canvas; 24″ x 36″
Jay Johnson America's Folk
Heritage Gallery

*Following page:* Larry Zingale
*The Puppy Crook*
1981
Oil on canvas; 12″ x 16″
Collection of Werner and
Karen Gundersheimer

335

# Bibliography

This selected bibliography lists the books and catalogs that were used in the preparation of this work as well as numerous publications that provide an overview of the range of folk art scholarship.

"American Eagle." *The American Way* (July-August 1969).

*American Folk Sculpture, the Personal and the Eccentric.* Bloomfield Hills, Mich.: Cranbrook Academy of Art Galleries, 1971.

*American Folk Sculpture, the Work of Eighteenth and Nineteenth Century Craftsmen.* Newark, N.J.: Newark Museum, 1931.

*American Paintings and Sculpture.* Newark, N.J.: Newark Museum, 1944.

*American Provincial Paintings from the Collection of J. Stuart Halladay and Herrel George Thomas* (exhibition catalog). New York: Whitney Museum of American Art, 1942.

Ames, Kenneth L. *Beyond Necessity: Art in the Folk Tradition.* Winterthur, Del.: Winterthur Museum, 1977.

Anderson, Marna Brill. *Selected Masterpieces of New York State Folk Painting* (exhibition catalog). New York: Museum of American Folk Art, 1977.

Andrews, Ruth, ed. *How to Know American Folk Art: Eleven Experts Discuss Many Aspects of the Field.* New York: E. P. Dutton, 1977.

*The Art of the Spanish Southwest.* Introduction by R. L. Scholkolp. Washington, D.C.: Index of American Design, n.d.

Bahti, Tom. *Southwestern Indian Ceremonials.* Las Vegas, Nevada: KC Publications, 1970.

Bearden, Romare, and Henderson, Harry. *Six Black Masters of American Art.* Zenith Books. Garden City, N.Y.: Doubleday & Co., 1972.

Belknap, Waldron Phoenix, Jr. *American Colonial Painting: Materials for a History.* Cambridge, Mass.: Harvard University Press, Belknap Press, 1959.

Bennett, Ian. *A History of American Painting.* London: Hamlyn Publishing Group, 1973.

Bilhalji-Merin, Oto. *Masters of Naive Art: A History and World Wide Survey.* New York: McGraw-Hill & Co., 1971.

Bishop, Robert. *American Folk Sculpture.* New York: E. P. Dutton, 1974.

————. *Folk Painters of America.* New York: E. P. Dutton, 1979.

Black, Mary, and Lipman, Jean. *American Folk Painting.* New York: Clarkson N. Potter, 1966.

Borneman, Henry S. *Pennsylvania German Illuminated Manuscripts.* New York: Dover Publications, 1973.

Boyd, E. *The Literature of Santos.* Dallas, Tex.: Southern Methodist University Press, 1950.

————. *The New Mexico Santero.* Santa Fe, N.M.: Museum of New Mexico, 1972.

————. *New Mexico Santos: How to Name Them.* Santa Fe, N.M.: Museum of New Mexico, 1966.

————. *Popular Arts of Spanish New Mexico.* Santa Fe, N.M.: Museum of New Mexico, 1974.

Bradshaw, Elinor Robinson. "American Folk Art in the Collection of The Newark Museum." *The Museum News Series,* vol. 19 (Summer-Fall 1967).

Burgess, Robert H. *Scrimshaw, The Whaleman's Art.* Newport News, Va.: Mariners Museum, n.d.

Cahill, Holger. *American Folk Art: The Art of the Common Man in America 1750-1900.* New York: W. W. Norton & Co. for the Museum of Modern Art, 1932.

————. *American Primitives, An Exhibit of the Paintings of Nineteenth Century Folk Artists.* Newark, N.J.: Newark Museum, 1930.

Cahill, Holger; Gauthier, Maximilien; Cassou, Jean; *et al. Masters of Popular Painting: Modern Primitives of Europe and America.* New York: Arno Press for the Museum of Modern Art, 1932, 1966.

Cain, Thomas: "Santos: Record of a Way of Life Now Gone." *Arizona Highways* (September 1955).

Cardinal, Roger. *Outsider Art.* New York: Praeger Publishers, 1972.

Carlisle, Lilian Baker. *18th and 19th Century American Art at Shelburne Museum.* Shelburne, Vt.: Shelburne Museum, 1961.

Carraher, Ronald G. *Artists in Spite of Art.* New York: Van Nostrand Reinhold, 1970.

*Carved by Prayer.* Spooner, Wis.: Museum of Woodcarving, n.d.

*Catalogue of the Initial Loan Exhibition.* New York: Museum of Early American Folk Art, 1962.

Chase, Judith Wragge. *Afro-American Art and Craft.* New York: Van Nostrand Reinhold, 1971.

Christensen, Erwin O. *Index of American Design.* New York: Macmillan, 1959.

————. *Early American Wood Carving.* New York: Dover Publications, 1972.

Craven, Wayne. *Sculpture in America.* New York: Thomas Y. Crowell Co., 1968.

Cummings, Abbott Lowell. *Rural Household Inventories 1675-1775.* Boston: The Society for the Preservation of New England Antiquities, 1964.

Davidson, Marshall. *The American Heritage History of Colonial Antiques.* New York: American Heritage Publishing Co., 1967.

————. *The American Heritage History of American Antiques from the Revolution to the Civil War.* New York: American Heritage Publishing Co., 1968.

————. *The American Heritage History of Antiques from the Civil War to World War I.* New York: American Heritage Publishing Co., 1969.

Dewhurst, C. Kurt; MacDowell, Betty; and MacDowell, Marsha. *Artists in Aprons. Folk Art by American Women* (exhibition catalog). New York: E. P. Dutton with the Museum of American Folk Art, 1979.

Dickey, Roland F. *New Mexico Village Arts.* Albuquerque, N.M.: University of New Mexico Press, 1970.

*Discoveries in American Folk Art.* New York: John Gordon Gallery, 1973.

Dockstader, Frederick J. *The Kachina and the White Man.* Cranbrook Institute of Science, Bulletin No. 35. Bloomfield Hills, Mich., 1954.

Dover, Cedric. *American Negro Art.* Greenwich, Conn.: New York Graphic Society, 1960.

Drepperd, Carl W. *American Pioneer Arts and Artists.* Springfield, Mass.: Pond-Ekberg Co., 1942.

Dresser, Louisa. *XVIIth Century Painting in*

New England (exhibition catalog). Worcester, Mass.: Worcester Art Museum, 1935.

Dunlap, William. A History of the Rise and Progress of the Arts of Design in the United States. 1834. Reprint. New York: Dover Publications, 1969.

Earnest, Adele. The Art of the Decoy. New York: Clarkson N. Potter, 1965.

Eaton, Allen H. Handicrafts of the Southern Highlands. New York: Russell Sage Foundation, 1937.

Ebert, John, and Ebert, Katherine. American Folk Painters. New York: Charles Scribner's Sons, 1975.

Ericson, John T., ed. Folk Art in America. Painting and Sculpture. New York: Mayflower Books. 1979.

Exhibition of American Folk Painting in Connection with the Massachusetts Tercentenary Celebration. Cambridge, Mass.: Harvard Society for Contemporary Art, 1930.

Feld, Stuart P. American Paintings for Public and Private Collections. New York: Hirschl & Adler, 1967.

Fischer, Ernst. The Necessity of Art. Translated by Anna Bastock. Baltimore, Md.: Pelican Books, 1964.

Fitzgerald, Ken. Weathervanes and Whirligigs. New York: Clarkson N. Potter, 1967.

Flower, Milton E. Wilhelm Schimmel and Aaron Mountz, Wood Carvers. Williamsburg, Va.: Abby Aldrich Rockefeller Folk Art Collection, 1965.

Folk Art and The Street of Shops. Dearborn, Mich.: Edison Institute, 1971.

Folk Art in America: A Living Tradition. Atlanta, Ga.: High Museum of Art, 1974.

Ford, Alice. Edward Hicks, Painter of the Peaceable Kingdom. Philadelphia: University of Pennsylvania Press, 1952.

———. Pictorial Folk Art, New England to California. New York and London: Studio Publications, 1949.

Frankenstein, Alfred. Angels over the Altar. Honolulu: University of Hawaii Press, 1961.

Fried, Frederick. A Pictorial History of the Carousel. New York: A. S. Barnes & Co., 1964.

———. Artists in Wood. New York: Clarkson N. Potter, 1970.

Friedman, Martin; Libertus, Ron; and Clark, Anthony M. American Indian Art: Form and Tradition. Walker Art Center, Indian Art Association, the Minneapolis Institute of Art. New York: E. P. Dutton, 1972.

Garbisch, Edgar William; Garbisch, Bernice Chrysler; et al. "American Primitive Painting, Collection of Edgar William and Bernice Chrysler Garbisch." Art in Amer-

ica, vol. 42, no. 2 (May 1954), special issue.

Gillon, Edmund V., Jr. Victorian Cemetery Art. New York: Dover Publications, 1972.

Girard, Alexander. Magic of a People: Folk Art and Toys from the Collection of the Girard Foundation. New York: Viking Press, 1968.

Goodrich, Lloyd, and Black, Mary. What Is American in American Art (exhibition catalog). New York: M. Knoedler, 1971.

Gordon, Leah. "Vanes of the Wind." Natural History (January 1972).

Gottesman, Rita Susswein. The Arts and Crafts in New York 1726–1776. New York: New-York Historical Society, 1938.

———. The Arts and Crafts of New York 1777–1799. New York: New-York Historical Society, 1954.

Gowans, Alan. Images of American Living. Philadelphia: J. B. Lippincott, 1964.

Groce, George C., and Wallace, David H. The New-York Historical Society's Dictionary of Artists in America, 1564–1860. New Haven: Yale University Press, 1957.

A Group of Paintings from the American Heritage Collection of Edith Kemper Jette and Ellerton Marcel Jette. Waterville, Me.: Colby College Press, 1956.

Harris, Neil, ed. The Land of Contrasts 1880–1901. New York: George Braziller, 1970.

Hemphill, Herbert W., Jr. Folk Sculpture USA (exhibition catalog). Brooklyn, N.Y.: Brooklyn Museum, 1976.

———, and Weissman, Julia. Twentieth-Century American Folk Art and Artists. New York: E. P. Dutton, 1974.

Hill, Ralph Nading, and Carlisle, Lilian Baker. The Story of the Shelburne Museum. Shelburne, Vt.: Shelburne Museum, 1960.

Holdridge, Barbara C., and Holdridge, Lawrence B. Ammi Phillips, Portrait Painter 1788–1865. New York: Clarkson N. Potter, 1969.

Hopmans, Susan. The Great Murals of Farmer John Brand, Clougherty Meat Packing Co. in Vernon, California. Photographs by Peter Kenner. New York: Colorcraft Lithographers, 1971.

Hornung, Clarence P. Treasury of American Design, 2 vols. New York: Harry N. Abrams, n.d.

Horwitz, Elinor Lander. Contemporary American Folk Artists. Philadelphia: J. B. Lippincott, 1975.

Hudson Valley Paintings 1700–1750 in the Albany Institute of History and Art. New York: Albany Institute of History and Art, 1959.

Illustrated Catalogue and Price List of Copper

Weather Vanes and Finials Manufactured by J. W. Fiske. New York: Gerald Kornblau Antiques, 1964.

Janis, Sidney. They Taught Themselves: American Primitive Painters of the Twentieth Century. New York: Dial Press, 1942.

The John and Mable Ringling Museum of Art. Orlando, Fla.: Hannau Robinson, 1971.

Jones, Agnes Halsey. Rediscovered Painters of Upstate New York, 1700–1875. Utica, N.Y.: Munson-Williams-Proctor Institute, 1958.

———, and Jones, Louis C. New-Found Folk Art of the Young Republic. Cooperstown, N.Y.: New York State Historical Association, 1960.

Jones, Louis C. "The Genre in American Folk Art." Papers on American Art. John C. Milley, ed. Maple Shade, N.J.: Edinburgh Press, 1976.

Kallir, Otto. Art and Life of Grandma Moses. New York: Gallery of Modern Art, 1969.

———, ed. Grandma Moses, My Life's History. New York: Harper & Row, 1952.

Kane, John. Sky Hooks: The Autobiography of John Kane. Notes and postscript by Mary McSwigan. Philadelphia: J. B. Lippincott, 1938.

Kaufman, Henry. Pennsylvania Dutch American Folk Art, 1946; rev. ed., New York: Dover Publications, 1964.

Ketchum, William C., Jr. American Folk Art: The View from New York (exhibition catalog). New York: Museum of American Folk Art and the Nassau County Museum of Fine Arts, 1980.

———. Western Memorabilia. Maplewood, N.J.: Hammond, 1980.

Laliberte, Norman, and Jones, Maureen. Wooden Images. New York: Reinhold Publishing Co., 1966.

Larkin, Oliver W. Art and Life in America, 1949; rev. ed., New York: Holt, Rinehart and Winston, 1960.

Lichten, Francis. Folk Art of Rural Pennsylvania. New York: Charles Scribner's Sons, 1946.

———. Pennsylvania Dutch Folk Art from the Geesey Collection and Others. New York: Metropolitan Museum of Art, 1958.

Lipman, Jean. American Folk Art. New York: Pantheon Books, 1948.

———. American Primitive Painting. New York: Oxford University Press, 1942. Reprint. New York: Dover Publications, 1972.

———. Pennsylvania Dutch Folk Arts. Philadelphia: Philadelphia Museum of Art, n.d.

———. Provocative Parallels. New York: Dutton Paperbacks, 1975.

———, ed. What Is American in American

*Art?* New York: McGraw-Hill Book Co., 1963.

————, and Winchester, Alice, eds. *Primitive Painters in America 1750–1950.* New York: Dodd, Mead, 1950. Reprint, Freeport, N.Y.: Books for Libraries Press, 1971.

Little, Nina Fletcher. *The Abby Aldrich Rockefeller Folk Art Collection.* Williamsburg, Va.: Colonial Williamsburg, 1957. Distributed by Little, Brown & Co.

————. *American Decorative Wall Painting 1700–1851.* New York: Dutton Paperbacks, 1972.

————. *Country Art in New England, 1790–1840.* Sturbridge, Mass.: Old Sturbridge Village, 1960.

————. *Land and Seascape as Observed by the Folk Artist.* Williamsburg, Va.: Colonial Williamsburg, 1969.

————. *New England Provincial Artists, 1775–1800.* Boston: Museum of Fine Arts, 1976.

*The Living Museum.* Springfield, Ill.: Illinois State Museum (November-December 1971).

Lord, Priscilla S., and Foley, Daniel J. *The Folk Arts and Crafts of New England.* Philadelphia: Chilton Book Co., 1965.

Lowe, David G. "Wooden Delights." *American Heritage,* vol. XX, no. 1 (December 1968).

Ludwig, Allen I. *Graven Images.* Middletown, Conn.: Wesleyan University Press, 1966.

Mackey, William J., Jr. *American Bird Decoys.* New York: E. P. Dutton, 1965.

"Made for the Season." *Art in America,* vol. 55 (1967).

Marquand, John P. *Timothy Dexter Revisited.* Boston: Little, Brown and Co., 1960.

Mather, Christine. "The Arts of the Spanish in New Mexico." *Antiques,* vol. 113, no. 2 (February 1978).

*The Metal of the State.* New York: Museum of American Folk Art, 1973.

*Missing Pieces: Georgia Folk Art 1770–1976.* Atlanta, Ga.: Georgia Council for the Arts and Humanities, 1976.

*M. & M. Karolik Collection of American Paintings 1815–1865 for the Museum of Fine Arts, Boston.* Essay by John I. H. Baur. Cambridge, Mass.: Harvard University Press for the Museum of Fine Arts, Boston, 1949.

*M. & M. Karolik Collection of American Watercolors and Drawings 1800–1875* (exhibition catalog). 2 vols. Boston: Museum of Fine Arts, 1962.

Muller, Nancy C. *Paintings and Drawings at the Shelburne Museum.* Shelburne, Vt.: Shelburne Museum, 1976.

Mundt, Ernest. *Art, Form, and Civilization.* Berkeley, Calif.: University of California Press, 1972.

Neal, Avon, and Parker, Ann. *Ephemeral Folk Figures.* New York: Clarkson N. Potter, 1969.

"The Newark Museum Collection and Exhibition, 1959–69." *The Museum News Series,* vol. 21 (Summer-Fall 1969).

*Nineteenth-Century Folk Painting: Our Spirited National Heritage* (selections from the collection of Mr. and Mrs. Peter H. Tillou). Storrs, Conn.: University of Connecticut, William Benton Museum of Art, 1973.

*101 American Primitive Watercolors and Pastels from the Collection of Edgar William and Bernice Chrysler Garbisch.* Washington, D.C.: National Gallery of Art, n.d.

*101 Masterpieces of American Primitive Painting from the Collection of Edgar William and Bernice Chrysler Garbisch.* New York: American Federation of Arts, 1961, New York: Doubleday & Co., 1962.

*Peabody Museum of Salem.* Salem, Mass.: Peabody Museum of Salem, 1969.

Pinckney, Pauline A. *Painting in Texas.* Austin, Tex.: University of Texas Press, 1967.

Read, Herbert. *The Meaning of Art.* New York: Praeger Publishers, 1972.

————. *Art Now.* New York: Pitman Publishing Corp., 1968.

————. *The Origins of Form in Art.* New York: Horizon Press, 1900.

————. *Art and Society.* London: Faber and Faber, 1956.

Rhodes, Lynette I. *American Folk Art from the Traditional to the Naive* (exhibition catalog). Cleveland: Cleveland Museum of Art, 1978.

Richardson, Edgar P. *Painting in America: The Story of 450 Years.* New York: Thomas Y. Crowell, 1956.

Robinson, Frederick B. *Somebody's Ancestors, Paintings by Primitive Artists of the Connecticut Valley* (exhibition catalog). Springfield, Mass.: Museum of Fine Arts, 1942.

Ross, Marjorie Drake. *The Book of Boston.* New York: Hastings House Publishers, 1960.

Sams, Henry W., ed. *Autobiography of Brook Farm.* Englewood Cliffs, N.J.: Prentice-Hall, 1958.

*Santos.* Fort Worth, Tex.: Amon Carter Museum of Western Art, 1964.

Savage, Gail; Savage, Norbert H.; and Sparks, Esther. *Three New England Watercolor Painters.* Chicago: Art Institute, 1974.

Schaefer-Simmern, Henry. *The Unfolding of Artistic Activity.* Berkeley, Calif.: University of California Press, 1970.

Sears, Clara Endicott. *Some American Primitives: A Study of New England Faces and Folk Portraits.* Boston: Houghton Mifflin, 1941.

Shalkop, Robert L. *Wooden Saints: The Santos of New Mexico.* Colorado Springs, Colo.: Taylor Museum of the Colorado Springs Fine Arts Center, 1967.

Shelley, Donald A. *The Fraktur-Writings or Illuminated Manuscripts of the Pennsylvania Germans.* Allentown, Pa.: Pennsylvania German Folklore Society, 1961.

Smith, Yvonne Brault. "Bellamy—Carver of Eagles." *National Antiques Review* (October 1972).

Stebbins, Theodore E. *American Master Drawings and Watercolors.* New York: Harper & Row, 1976.

Stein, Roger B. *Seascape and the American Imagination.* New York: Clarkson N. Potter, 1975.

Stevens, Alfred. "The Images." *Yankee Magazine* (July 1969).

Stitt, Susan. *Museum of Early Southern Decorative Arts in Old Salem.* Winston-Salem, N.C.: Museum of Early Southern Decorative Arts, 1970.

Stoudt, John J. *Early Pennsylvania Arts and Crafts.* New York: A. S. Barnes & Co., 1964.

Tavares, M. A. "Scrimshaw, The Art of The Whaleman." *National Antiques Review* (February 1972).

Todd, A. L., and Weisbord, Dorothy B. *Favorite Subjects in Western Art.* New York: Dutton Paperbacks, 1968.

Webster, David S., and Kehoe, William. *Decoys at Shelburne Museum.* Shelburne, Vt.: Shelburne Museum, 1961.

Welsh, Peter C. *American Folk Art, the Art and Spirit of a People.* Washington, D.C.: Smithsonian Institution, 1965.

"What Is American Folk Art. A Symposium." *Antiques,* vol. 57, no. 5 (May 1950).

*Where Liberty Dwells: 19th-Century Art by the American People.* Works of Art from the Collection of Mr. and Mrs. Peter Tillou (exhibition catalog). Privately published, 1976.

Wiggington, Eliot. *The Foxfire Book.* New York: Anchor Books, 1972.

Wilder, M. A. "Santos." *The American West* (Fall 1965).

Woodward, Richard B. *American Folk Painting from the Collection of Mr. and Mrs. William E. Wiltshire III* (exhibition catalog). Introduction by Mary Black Richmond: Virginia Museum, 1977.

# List of Illustrations